THE COMPLETE GUIDE ON HOW TO NEGOTIATE

Master the Art of Getting What You Want in Business and in Life

BY TALI RAPHAELY

MiMo

PRESS

MiMo

PRESS

ISBN: 0615783465
ISBN 13: 9780615783468
Library of Congress Control Number: 2013904970
Tali Raphaely
Baltimore, MD

CONTENTS

To my parents, Moshe and Miri. Everything I do in life is possible because of the support, love, guidance, and discipline I have always received from both of you.

Thank you for everything you have done for me and for Ron, Aurit, and Leeat. You have always done your best with us and we will appreciate it forever.

THE COMPLETE GUIDE ON HOW TO NEGOTIATE

Master the Art of Getting What You Want in Business and in Life

INTRODUCTION

I believe that life presents us with a series of negotiations. Further, I believe that it is your negotiation and your people skills that will ultimately determine how you live your life and how easily things work out for you. Imagine knowing how to get what you want in your life from interactions with friends, business associates, employees, your boss, clients, colleagues, store clerks, customer-service representatives, and complete strangers. Using the techniques I'm about to share, you will be able to consistently achieve the results you want when dealing with others.

For instance, what happens when you call a popular restaurant to make a reservation and it is fully booked? Unless you just give up and call another place, the manner in which you handle this situation is, in essence, a negotiation. The host on the telephone has something you want, which is the ability to approve your request. How do you get him or her to help you? Or how do you decide who picks the restaurant on your night out with friends? How do you and your husband split the household chores and responsibilities? Examples of negotiation in everyday life are endless. And it obviously goes without saying that you're definitely negotiating when asking for a raise, buying a car, selling your house, or working out pricing with a vendor or service provider.

My goal is to equip you with the negotiating skills to get more from everyday life—and reveal the philosophy behind these practices. First, you will learn the fundamentals, a way of thinking ahead and looking at a situation *before* you are in it, the basic tools and knowledge of leverage required to be a skilled negotiator. And when you are a *skilled* negotiator, you will get what you want when dealing with people while placing them in a position in which *they* get what *they* want as well. In later chapters you will learn how to refine your savvy and develop insight into analyzing differences, arguments, and confrontations in all types of give-and-take situations. I will enable you to see these situations from a new perspective that just about guarantees success.

As an experienced real estate attorney and owner of a recognized nationwide real estate title company, and also as a real estate investor and landlord, I have refined my negotiating skills in countless situations. I have bought income-producing rental properties, bought and sold real estate-based businesses, represented clients in contract, employment, and lease negotiations, and bargained lease terms with countless tenants and landlords. I have also negotiated salaries and raise requests with hundreds of employees. Additionally, I have negotiated costs and fees with thousands of clients, independent contractors, and vendors. I learned and honed my skills "hands-on." While others often view the negotiation process as intimidating and frustrating, I have always embraced it as an enjoyable challenge.

The thousands of opportunities I've had over the years to be involved in so many different types of negotiations have resulted in my ability to direct and perfect the negotiation process time after time. The experience I have obtained through years of negotiating, my optimistic perspective, and my ability to analyze and understand people, their choice of words, their reactions, their body language, and their overall demeanor, have allowed me to excel at this very important skill. I also greatly enjoy inspiring, motivating, and sharing my experiences with other people. As a result, I find it only natural to want to share my insight and strategies with you. It would provide me with much pride and joy to know that individuals apply my techniques and are successful in their negotiations as a result.

What I have learned from my many experiences is that in order to get what you want in life you have to appreciate that just about everything is negotiable. I am confident that my advice will help you in learning just how to negotiate in life. So, let's begin.

CHAPTER ONE

The Tale of Sad Sam and Skillful Sam

Let's begin by imagining what it would be like for Sam if he lacks the skills to negotiate. Therefore, let's talk about Sad, Skill-free Sam, just for purposes of telling a story.

It's 7 a.m. on Monday morning, and Sam is starting a relatively typical day in his life. He and his wife are trying to wake up their kids for school, but, as usual, their kids want to stay in bed. The struggle continues for a while until he has had enough of it and leaves the situation to his wife. He knows that she's going to be angry at him for giving up, but he decides there's nothing more he can do. Before he leaves the house, however, he also manages to engage in a quick skirmish with her about where the family will go on vacation this year. He wants to go somewhere quiet so he can relax, while she wants to go where there will be many activities for family participation. This year will probably end up like every year prior and they will fight about this particular topic until someone just gets too tired and gives up, agreeing to a trip that no one can enjoy.

As Sam gets into his car to drive to the office, his landscaper approaches him in his front yard. The landscaper explains that his costs—gas, labor—have gone up and he needs to raise his fees from $200 to $250 per week, which means Sam's lawn expenses just went up over $2,500 per year in one conversation! He grudgingly agrees to this price increase, as he believes there's nothing he can do about it.

When he gets to his office he realizes he still hasn't called to make the dinner reservation he was asked two weeks ago to take care of for this upcoming Thursday night. He and his wife are supposed to be going to dinner at a posh restaurant with three other couples to celebrate a friend's birthday. Sam gets very nervous now because he knows he has a better chance of winning the lottery than getting a reservation at the city's trendiest and most in-demand restaurant. Sure enough, when he calls he is told there's no way they can fit in a party of eight people *this* Thursday night. He believes there's nothing he can do about this now, so he hangs up the phone, thinking about how upset his wife and friends are going to be when he shares the bad news with them.

After a couple of minutes go by, he realizes one of his employees is standing in front of him. Sam is a supervisor in an office-supply company. Twenty people report directly to him, and he reports directly to the president. He's been promising to discuss with this employee her request for a raise. He knows she's deserving of one, and that she's been patient with her requests. He also knows that five other employees are also requesting raises at this time, but he is working with a limited budget. He doesn't know what to do because he doesn't want to lose any of these very dedicated employees, but he also can't afford to give each employee what he or she is requesting. Consequently, he's been stalling, which is only compounding this particular employee's frustration; Sam tells her once again that he will get back to her.

He goes to see the president to discuss the possibility of increasing his budget to deal with this situation. He is informed that there is just *no way* that the budget could be increased any time soon. He has no choice but to accept the decision. He tells himself that any attempts to try to change the president's mind would just be a waste of his time, as she is very stubborn and extremely intimidating.

Later, while on a conference call, he can't help but get aggravated because it's so hot, as the air-conditioning in the office hasn't worked for two weeks. There's been an ongoing debate among his company, the landlord, and the air-conditioning vendor under contract regarding whose responsibility it is to pay the costs of fixing it.

Before he leaves the office for the day, he speaks briefly with the elderly couple that is selling a vacation home he's interested in buying. He really wants to work things out with them since he's always wanted a vacation home just like this one, and the price seems to be fair. He still thinks, however, that they should lower their price because of some of the issues brought up by the home inspector he hired. As much as he would love to buy this house, he has recently realized that it's probably just not going to happen because it doesn't seem likely they'll be able to work out all of their differences.

He eventually makes it back home that evening. Beaten down pretty badly already, he stands no chance of winning the war of the remote control with his wife. He finally heads to bed, grateful that this day is finally coming to an end, although he realizes that tomorrow will probably be very similar.

While reading the above scenario, did you realize how many hidden opportunities to rearrange the situations to his satisfaction Sad Sam avoided on this typical day? Every one of these many situations involved a negotiation that Sad Sam felt unequipped to deal with, so he sidestepped and merely avoided what will continue to be issues most likely not resolved to his satisfaction.

If you want to continue letting life happen to you rather than *for* you, follow Sad Sam's example. But if you are ready to recognize that every situation or problem offers a chance to negotiate things to turn out your way, read on! You are in control of your life, and you're in control of how most situations that affect you turn out. The key is being able to deal with people, see things from their perspective, and understand their wants and needs. With insight and practice, these instances become opportunities to exercise your people skills, communication skills, reasoning skills, and problem-solving skills.

Intrigued? Confused? Excited?

Begin the journey of becoming a skilled negotiator. Let us now revisit the day from the perspective of Skillful Sam.

Skillful Sam recognizes that the daily struggle to wake up and activate his kids starts each day with unnecessary stress. It's time to negotiate this situation to his liking. After all, they're just kids and, more importantly, they're his kids, and he loves them dearly. Are there certain things they've been asking for—a trip somewhere, a toy, or permission to take on a new freedom? Why not negotiate with his kids, promising them one of these things in return for their promise to get up on time every morning with no hassles? Now he's given them incentive to make his life more peaceful, as well as a goal for them to work toward!

How about the battle over the family trip? A skilled negotiator understands that when you are trying to work out a situation, you must think creatively about options that may not come up at first thought. His mind begins to race as he considers all of the interesting ways in which he can settle the differences he and his wife have over travel plans. Is there no place on earth to which they could conveniently travel that could provide each of them with what they want in a vacation? Aren't there plenty of destinations that offer quiet, peaceful areas while also providing other areas within the destination for activities and more excitement? Can't they split up for a couple of hours on some days so they each do more of what they want? Or can't his wife take part in water sports and other adventures while he relaxes at the pool close by? How about alternating vacation preferences? If time and money are factors, as they are for most of us, have they considered taking two shorter trips instead of one long trip? Regardless of how he resolves this situation, do you see how thinking outside the box and working together to find creative solutions opens up so many possibilities for solving problems?

Sam's landscaping bill has just gone up $2,500 per year in an instant. Or has it? Skillful Sam certainly wouldn't agree to spend all of that additional money so quickly without trying to figure out an alternative. What if he refers the landscaper to two of his neighbors and, if the neighbors become new clients, then the landscaper will agree to keep his fees at the current price? Or can he think of something the landscaper does regularly as part of his landscaping that Skillful Sam really doesn't care about very much? Could they agree to let the side yard go natural? Or can he have the landscaper start coming once every ten days? Or can he tell the landscaper that he may have to find another landscaper if he must raise his price, and then wait and see if the landscaper decides that losing Sam as a customer isn't worth it? Once the landscaper is faced with the possibility of losing his customer, he may have a newfound appreciation for the weekly $200 revenue. Lastly, if none of these solutions works for him, can he consider making a counteroffer to the landscaper? Maybe he can negotiate some middle ground of $225 a week.

How is Skillful Sam going to avoid disappointing his wife and their friends because he forgot to make dinner reservations? The hostess has already said no, so at this point Skillful Sam recognizes he has nothing to lose by trying a different approach with her. The hostess has something he wants, which is the ability to approve his request or, if it's not in her hands, she can relay his request to the next level of management. How does he get her to help him? He could start by appealing to her sympathy and explaining the situation to her. He is in essence negotiating with her to help him in return for providing her with an opportunity to be a good person and to be helpful to a stranger in a tough situation. If he is a regular at this restaurant, he should make that known immediately. Can he joke around in a polite and fun manner, implying that her inability to help him could cause him to take his business to the restaurant's biggest competitor?

He could show his human side and attempt to connect with her in some manner. If she takes a liking to him or thinks he's a good guy she'll be more likely to go out of her way to help him.

He could admit he messed up and didn't follow through on his responsibility to make reservations when he should have done so, and try to share with her how upset and disappointed the others will be as a result. If he's been kind, funny, patient, entertaining, or polite throughout his conversation with this hostess, she may decide to help him. He also thinks of the possibility of offering her a gift or a cash tip in return for her to squeeze them in or at least to advance a plea on his behalf to management.

If all of this fails, he still doesn't give up. His never-say-die attitude encourages him to ask to speak with the manager or some other person in charge who may be more willing to help him. He realizes that he's getting nowhere with the hostess, so he figures he has nothing to lose by trying his case with someone new. Additionally, he's aware of the small possibility that, if he makes this request respectfully, maybe the hostess just helps him because he's been nice to her and appreciates how much he needs her assistance. If he speaks with the manager, he goes through the same type of strategies with the manager, again making sure to be very respectful and polite while arguing for his cause.

If this doesn't work, he will immediately start thinking about a backup plan. He may begin to lobby his wife and friends to try a different place instead, doing his best to convince them of the superior benefits of the new restaurant. Ultimately, he will turn this negative into a positive, making sure the dinner is a great experience for everyone.

After Sam hangs up the telephone, he addresses the situation with his employee who has been requesting a raise. He knows she deserves it, he wants to make her happy, and he wants to do what he can to keep her with the company. He also knows his boss is tough to deal with, but he decides he needs to convince her to do something for this employee. He speaks with his boss and explains that the company cannot afford to lose this employee. His boss reminds him of their budgetary concerns, but he has already anticipated this response and he's ready to make his case. He wisely demonstrates the revenue this employee directly brings in to the company, explains her unique skills, and compares these factors with how much she's costing the company in salary. The numbers speak for themselves and his boss sees clearly that not making this employee happy could end up costing the company significant lost revenue in the long run. She agrees that it would be wise to grant the raise, but they still need to figure out how to make the numbers work. He asks her if he can look over the budget so they can decide together what adjustments they can make so that additional money is available for the salary increase. Having made these adjustments, they decide they can now afford to give the employee a raise.

Back at his desk, he finds he's sweating badly as a result of the broken air-conditioning, so he calls the landlord in an attempt to resolve the issue. Knowing he has nothing to lose by trying, he asks the landlord what it would take to get them to straighten this out without passing the financial responsibility onto his company or the air-conditioning company. The landlord reminds him that his company's lease expires in two months and that the landlord has been trying to get Skillful Sam's CFO to renew for another three years. Skillful Sam knows that his company has no intention of leaving and that they just have been too busy lately to finalize renewing the lease. But the landlord doesn't know this and, as a result, seems to be nervous about whether they're staying. Skillful Sam immediately sees this as an opportunity to gain an edge in this negotiation.

He explains that they really like the building, but this situation with the air-conditioning has given them doubts lately. They can't consider renewing the lease until they know the air-conditioning is completely fixed, since the heat has been hurting productivity. He does an excellent job of convincing the landlord to see the big picture.

Skillful Sam is having a pretty good day so far, wouldn't you say? He lets his mind turn to the vacation home he wants to buy from the elderly couple. He reminds himself of the main issues that have been preventing the parties from working out a deal: price, fixtures, and time frame. He understands that a big part of working differences out is the ability to compromise and that sometimes having several issues of contention actually makes coming together easier because there are more opportunities to compromise. For example, Skillful Sam may be especially concerned about price because he has limited funds available. The sellers might be more concerned with being able to take their fixtures with them because of sentimental value. Or they may be more focused on the time frame because they need additional time to prepare for their move. They are making major changes to their lives because this is their residence, while Skillful Sam is only planning to use the house as a vacation home. Maybe the sellers would be willing to lower the price significantly, if he gives in on the other two issues. All he has to do is have an open and productive conversation with the sellers, assess priorities for each side, and they can work together toward common ground.

When Skillful Sam gets home that evening, he's in a great mood and is happy to see his family. He decides it's time to utilize his superb negotiation and people skills to work something out with his wife regarding the battle of the remote control. He begins thinking of all of the variables involved that are relevant to this situation. He sees many different ways to compromise, and he also sees other unrelated issues that can be brought into negotiations to form package deals. He sees the big picture, doesn't focus too narrowly on any one issue, and thinks of many multiple options to arrive at a satisfactory result for all parties.

This concludes the tale of how two people handled identical situations in very different manners. One goes through life frustrated, unhappy, and defeated. The other always seems to be able to work things out. The only difference is having command of the proper skills to negotiate a path through life's challenging events.

I want to empower you with this ability to turn dead-end situations with no apparent possible solution into promising, rewarding, and positive opportunities with multiple possible solutions. This can be done without being manipulative, dishonest, or confrontational. Instead, my techniques foster respect, courtesy, and cooperation. Read on to learn how to master the art of getting what you want in business and in life!

CHAPTER TWO

Getting Started with Some Basic Concepts

The basic concepts in this chapter are fairly obvious and straightforward, but they must be addressed at the outset for the sake of clarity and completeness.

1. Good Cop/Bad Cop

Sometimes it can be very helpful to present the appearance that you have a spouse, an attorney, an accountant, a partner, or an associate with whom you may have to consult from time to time during or at the very end of the negotiation. This technique provides you with many benefits. It allows you to buy time to think through and analyze an offer. You simply say, "Please excuse me while I check with my associate," or, if you want to buy even more time, you could say, "Please let me consult with my associate and then get back to you." It's a simple and acceptable way to create additional time to think, compare other offers, obtain additional information, or keep the other side in suspense. It also allows you to place the blame on someone else even if you're the one actually asking for a concession. "I would love to accept, but my colleague has already told me she won't be okay with that. She's pretty tough and not always the easiest person with whom to deal. Can you improve your offer *just a bit* and I'll try to reason with her?"

The good cop/bad cop routine is a strategy named after a well-known police tactic used on suspected criminals during interrogations. One cop is friendly and comforting and makes the accused feel safe, while the other cop is accusatory and demanding.

You are the reasonable cop, so the other party won't get angry with you. You *want* to get this deal *done.* You're asking for these concessions because your less reasonable associate—the bad cop—is insisting on them. You say to the other party, "We're so close to working this out now, let's not let these last little requests ruin the deal when we've come so far." It's very helpful to be able to blame someone else whom the other party can't even speak with, so use this tactic when applicable and possible.

2. Negotiate with the Person Who Has the Final Authority

If you aren't dealing with the right individual, you will be subject to constant frustration when the person you are speaking with has to consult with someone else every time you try to get a concession. You may even begin to feel like you're bidding against yourself, because your concessions will come quickly while theirs will occur more slowly because of additional communication with a third party. If you realize more than one person is involved in the negotiation, try to negotiate with both of them together at the same time. You would ask something like, "Can we get Sally to join us in these discussions so that we are all together and this process can go much more smoothly?"

Whether that additional individual really exists or whether the other party is pretending that person is involved, essentially the good cop/bad cop technique is now being used against you. You can bring it up jokingly, but make sure they're aware that you know what's going on. Raise the issue carefully to avoid offense. You could say something like, "I'm usually the one who is using the good cop/bad cop routine on others—it's not as much fun when it's being used on me!" When they know you have recognized the tactic, they'll realize it's not going to work this time.

3. Power in Numbers

Think big to move things forward. Can you offer to buy in bulk? Can you demonstrate you can provide them with more customers? Can you partner up with anyone else in this transaction so that you have more buying power?

4. Pigs Get Fat, Hogs Get Slaughtered

It's good to be motivated, to hustle and strive to get a good deal, but when you become too greedy you end up upsetting the other person, thereby forcing him or her to explore other options. Be confident in your position, but never get careless and think the other side has no options. Rarely is what you are offering so unique, special, or different that the other person has no leverage. Your offer may have been a first choice, but if you back someone far enough into a corner you'd be surprised how creative and resourceful he or she can be. If you are too unrealistic, demanding, or insulting, or if you do anything else to cause your counterparts to feel trapped or discontented, they are going to do everything in their power to go deal with someone else. Don't push too hard. Be sensitive to detecting another person's boundaries.

5. Understand Your Disadvantage

Whoever needs or wants the deal the most starts from a position of weakness. This doesn't mean you can't use your negotiating skills to reduce this impact, or even the odds, but understand that if you want his car more than he wants to sell it to you, then you are starting off at a disadvantage. It's okay, because it's reality, but be honest with yourself. You may end up not getting the deal of the century, but your aim must be to reduce the other side's advantage as much as possible.

6. Doing or Saying Nothing May Be Your Best Choice

Be patient. When you are unsure what to say, say nothing; when you are unsure what to do, do nothing. You can't take back what you say or do. Sometimes it's best to give yourself some time to digest information or think things through before reacting too quickly.

7. Good Things Come to Those Who Wait

Don't let yourself be forced into making quick decisions or doing number crunching faster than you are comfortable doing. Take your time, excuse yourself, gather your thoughts, do some math on a piece of paper, and think through what you want to say. Don't be paranoid about having to step away at times.

Depending on the circumstances, walking away for several minutes may not be enough. If it involves a bigger decision or requires more thought, then sleep on it. Never be impulsive, always be patient during negotiations. Patience usually pays off. Often a negotiation goes through stages lasting over several conversations or days. Sometimes it's easier for the other side to make adjustments over time rather than meeting your desired number in one conversation. Allow breathing space, time for things to evolve. Keep in mind that people don't like to feel that they have wasted their time. The more time the other side spends negotiating with you, the more they will be motivated to make concessions to get the deal done. They have become invested in a positive outcome.

8. Speak from the Perspective of the Other Person

Remember, to be a skilled negotiator, you have to perceive the negotiation and the complete situation from the other person's perspective and not your own. The better you become at seeing things from her eyes, the better you will be able to help solve her problems and meet her needs.

The unskilled negotiator meets with a potential client and says, "Getting your business will mean so much to our company. It will allow us to beat last year's numbers and we'll have you to thank for that!" How likely is it that the client cares about your numbers—unless he or she sees a personal benefit in doing so?

The skilled negotiator learns about the client's wants and needs ahead of time and speaks about them. You say something like, "If you buy these products, your productivity will go up 50 percent, while your costs will go down 25 percent." You are now speaking to the client from their perspective.

9. Communicate Effectively

Make sure the other side understands your points and concerns. When you bring up your ideas, rebuttals, objections, or resolutions to the other side, you have to make sure they have listened and understood. How can you convince them of anything if they don't understand you? When you rebut a point made or raise any objections, you have to make sure your reasoning is crystal clear to your counterpart.

10. Prepare in Case Things Change Later

When possible and applicable, negotiate an exit strategy for yourself into the terms of the deal. People often assume that everything will work out as the parties had hoped, but in reality things change with time. A wise negotiator, however, always leaves himself or herself with as many "outs" as possible while being careful not to anger or offend the other side.

An example of an "out" would be negotiating for an inspection clause as part of a sales contract for a home you are purchasing, a home that wasn't your first choice. This creates an opportunity to change your mind about buying the house with no penalty within a certain number of days from the date of the inspection. What if the very next day after signing the contract the owner of your dream home calls you, offering to sell you that house instead? You've provided yourself with an easy "out" and you are able to walk away from the original deal. Another example would be an early termination clause in a lease. You may be very excited at the time you sign the lease, unable to imagine ever wanting to leave that new house you just rented, but you never know what may come up after you move in. Suppose it has unseen mold? Suppose it's haunted? It's always helpful to have some sort of "out," even if there's some penalty associated with that early termination. The penalty may still be a much better option than having to stay for the duration of the lease term.

11. Always Act in Good Faith

Even if you're not acting completely reasonably and the other party is getting frustrated with how things are going, you will continue to receive the benefit of the doubt from them as long as they see you are acting in good faith. Once you lose their trust, you will immediately be faced with a very closed-off and cynical person at the other end of the table. It becomes extremely difficult to come to an agreement under those conditions.

12. Do Your Homework

Do your research and know the facts as well as or better than the other party, because by failing to prepare you are preparing to fail. Know the market and what alternatives exist to this particular offer and how those alternatives may be similar or different from this one. If you are selling your car, have you done ample research on other similar cars so you are educated on its true worth? If you mistakenly believe your car to be worth more than it is, buyers will continue to pass on yours as they find others like it for less money. Alternatively, if you fail to do your homework on the true value of your car, you could *underestimate* the value and end up asking for and accepting less than you should have received.

13. Spread the Word

Don't take your own network for granted while you're involved or about to become involved in an important negotiation. Reach out to as many people as you can who may be able to provide you with relevant advice or lead you to others who could provide advice. Your boss may be close friends with the neighbors of the people whose house you're looking to buy. Your best friend's brother may work at the body shop that previously worked on that rare sports car you're thinking of buying. Your professor may know another student who has a condo to rent.

Use your network. Talk to people. You are no dummy for asking questions, but you are a dummy if you have a network and are too proud, stubborn, or lazy to use it.

14. Develop Appreciation for Getting a Good Deal

Learn to care about getting a good deal. The more you can get yourself to see the art and skill of negotiating as a challenge you want to excel at, the more likely you will continue to improve at it. Learn to enjoy the process and note how much more skillful you become each time you negotiate. If you don't enjoy the process, you will ultimately fail to get your way in your haste to get the deal done.

15. Perception is Reality

When appropriate in certain situations, create a perception of scarcity. People want what they can't have. At other times, consider creating the bandwagon effect. It is helpful when you can make statements like, "We've been getting a lot of calls about this item," or "We will have to get back to you because we have ten more interviews scheduled today for this position."

16. Be Confident

The more confident you appear—without being arrogant or cocky—the more difficult it is for the other person to say no. By the same reasoning, if you seem apologetic or doubtful that your request will be granted, it becomes much easier for the other person to say no. By appearing doubtful when making a request you are essentially demonstrating to the other person that he or she would be acting reasonably if he or she denied your offer or suggestion.

For instance, a particular buyer may say, "I know I'm probably asking for too much, but is there any way you would consider reducing your price by another fifty dollars?" Compare that with a more skillful buyer who may say, "Our numbers are very close now; if you reduce your price by another fifty dollars we should be able to work this out." Note how the first buyer made it obvious to the seller that his request was unreasonable, thereby making it easy for the seller to reject it while still feeling like he's acting reasonably. Compare that with the skillful buyer, who was *not* apologetic about his request and did not make it as easy for the seller to reject the offer.

17. Trust Your Instincts

Trust your instincts regarding people. Sometimes you develop a gut feeling about the integrity, character, or true motivations of an individual. Be open-minded, and give people a chance to prove you wrong, if your instincts about someone are not positive; however, stay aware of these gut feelings and give them the credit they deserve. If you don't trust someone, don't do business with them!

When in doubt, never forget the old fable of the scorpion and the frog. A scorpion is drowning in a river and asks a frog to help him and carry him to land. The frog refuses and says to the scorpion that he's afraid the scorpion will sting him before they even get to land. The scorpion convinces the frog that he won't sting him, stating that if he stung him the frog would sink and the scorpion would drown. The frog is convinced with this logic and carries the scorpion. Before they reach land, however, the scorpion stings the frog. As they both begin to drown, the frog asks the scorpion why he stung him. The scorpion responds:

"What did you think? I'm a scorpion. It's my nature."

Don't expect a scorpion to change its nature. If you suspect that someone is capable of being dishonest or deceitful, be on the lookout for past indications that this person is untrustworthy.

Besides trusting your instincts about any individual, also trust your instincts regarding the deal itself. As they say, if it seems too good to be true it probably is! When you are contemplating doing a deal, and it seems too good to be true, there is a weighing process you automatically conduct whether you realize it or not. Do I take a risk because I don't want to pass up an excellent opportunity, or do I walk away because I don't want to be scammed? Be prudent, do your due diligence on the people with whom you associate and on the deal you are weighing. Don't lose sight of the fact that there's no such thing as a free lunch. If you find yourself feeling like you are truly getting something for nothing, ask yourself why this is happening. Why is this person doing this for you? Is it love, friendship, or a sense of obligation? Could it be because they want something in return, whether it's now or later? Or is it possible that you are in fact getting scammed?

CHAPTER THREE

Talk Less, Listen More!

The following principles of verbal communication yield enormous power in every negotiation. Master these rules of when to speak and how to listen and you will come out on top every time.

1. Listen Carefully

This can't be stressed enough. Every single word the other party uses counts. Can you tell what the other person wants in this negotiation? What does he seem to focus on when speaking about the current situation? Are you paying close attention to his choice of words and the tone used? Do you sense desperation or urgency? Do you sense confidence in his position, or do you detect that he is aware his offer is too low? Are you picking up an apologetic tone in his offer? What he says and how he says it will help you in your negotiations.

2. Give Them the Silent Treatment

Don't be threatened by silence, and don't rush to fill uncomfortable silence with chatter. First, there is a good chance that you will say something that could end up hurting your position in the negotiation. Second, you may be taking away an opportunity to hear something the other party may be leading up to saying. It is very likely that the other party is probably feeling equally uneasy in periods of silence. Often it is during times of silence that one of the parties says something that tips the negotiation in the other's favor. Silence is your friend. Let the other party speak up first. Let them make that mistake or concession.

Let's assume a woman makes you an offer of twenty thousand dollars for your car. You can react, you can accept or reject her offer, or you can make a counteroffer. Any of those responses can wait a few additional moments. What would happen if you were just quiet for a little bit—just enough for an uncomfortable silence? It will seem to the other person like you're thinking about what she just said, you're weighing your options, or you're thinking of what to say next. But if a couple of extra seconds go by, she may begin to feel that uncomfortable silence taking over. She may blurt out something that could be very helpful to you. There's generally no harm in trying this, so it's always worth a shot.

Anytime a discussion is at a pivotal point is a good time to try the silence tactic. After what seems to her as a couple of seconds too long, she won't be able to help but think that *you're* thinking the same thing *she's* thinking. If she knows her offer is low, she will probably take your silence as an indication that you also think the offer is too low. She might break the silence and blurt out a new offer, a concession, or a justification for her price. The amazing thing is that now you've essentially got her bidding against herself without saying even one word!

Let's now assume that she's the seller and that you're

considering purchasing her car. Let's assume further that you've asked her whether the car has been in an accident. She responds that it has not, and now you decide to be silent. Remember, the other person is trying to figure out *why* you are being silent. She may interpret your silence as disbelief of her statement that the car had not been in an accident. What if the car actually had been in an accident and she was dishonest about it? The long silence may get to her and she may either be overcome with guilt for lying or sense that you suspect the truth. In that moment of uncomfortable silence, she may attempt to correct her last statement and say something like, "Actually, I just remembered the car was in a little fender-bender two years ago. It was so minor that I completely forgot about it until just now." Had you not initiated that moment of silence, the two of you would have quickly moved on to the next topic of discussion, and the truth would never have surfaced.

3. You Only Learn When the Other Person is Talking

Has anyone ever told you that you're not a good listener or that you talk too much? If there ever was a time to take heed of that advice, it is during negotiations. Let the other person talk as much as possible, and just sit back and listen. He may speak about his desired number. He may discuss his motivations or tell you something about himself, other offers, or about the item for which you are negotiating—if you simply let him keep talking. In a negotiation, make sure to do your best at all times to *get* more information than you *give*. You already know what you have to say, so you're only learning when the other party is talking.

People love to talk, especially about themselves, so why not take advantage of it? Ask questions often, especially if there's something you are trying to find out that could assist you in analyzing the situation.

4. Be Curious

Curiosity will get you far in the world of negotiations. You will learn valuable information when you ask questions. You won't receive complete information unless you ask for it.

5. Everything You Say Can Be Used Against You

Think before you say anything because how you open the door for a conversation could go in a certain direction without you even realizing it. You might mention a trivial detail that could lead to follow-up questions—and those could lead to information you did not wish to share.

For example, let's say you're interviewing for a job, and you have decided to omit from your resume a particular past job because you aren't very proud of how you handled yourself there. Maybe you were only there briefly and did not consider it worthy to include on your resume. Yet during your interview you accidentally mention something pertaining to that job. Perhaps the topic of different types of software comes up during your interview, and you make casual mention of a type of software you've used in the past. The problem is that the only job at which you actually used that software was that job you have omitted from your resume. If the individual interviewing you is interested in that type of software and now asks you what company you were working for when you used that software, how will you answer? You've just placed yourself between a rock and a hard place. Do you make yourself appear like an idiot by saying you don't remember the name of the company you worked for when using that software, or do you make yourself look disingenuous by now divulging the name of a company that you've left off your resume?

6. Objections Require You to Pay Close Attention to What the Other Side is Saying

Obviously, being a good listener is both polite and informational regarding the other party's desires, goals, or motivations. But there's still another reason to listen effectively: you have to be able to intelligently and effectively address any concerns, issues, or objections they may raise. Careful listening enables you to address their concerns *precisely*. If you didn't get the full gist of their objections, there's no way you can allay their fears.

7. Pause Before You Begin to Talk

It's rude to interrupt someone when he or she is speaking and, additionally, you want the speaker to finish his or her sentences, as you want to hear everything being said. You are learning about this person's goals, needs, and motivations. Why would you stop someone who is about to reach the punch line? Never assume you know what someone is about to say or the way the speaker will finish the sentence. *Be thankful for every word you get.* It is all helpful information. And pause before you reply, just in case the speaker is not done. He may reward you for your patience with a quick follow-up to his last statement, which sometimes is the exact moment he divulges additional useful information.

8. Listen for What is *Not* Said

Oftentimes, what the person doesn't say is even more important than what he or she does say. Based on the totality of the circumstances, try to ascertain why something was *not* said. Why did the people on the other side omit something you expected them to discuss? Why did they skip over a concept or issue that seems to be important? Why are they not insisting on something you believe they should require?

9. Ask Many Open-Ended Questions

You will learn much more from your counterparts on the other side if you get them to talk more, and there's no better way to learn from them than by asking questions. Standard yes/no questions give you just a glimpse into what someone is seeking. Ask open-ended questions and sit back, listen effectively, mirror their points, keep talking, and learn all you can about what they want and don't want, and why. If you are not sure how to ask an open-ended question, pay attention to how interviewers do it. They tend to avoid the questions that only require a yes or no answer.

10. Never Fail to Listen

Sometimes there's a tendency to be so overwhelmed with what you are saying, your beliefs, and your entire presentation that you tune out the other party. Have you ever believed in something so much that you were convinced everyone else would understand if they just shut up and listened to you, if they heard you explain it again? It's perfectly acceptable to believe strongly in your position, but you can't lose sight of the fact that everyone will not always agree with you or see things the way you do regardless of how loudly you speak or how many times you repeat yourself. What if the other side is just as obsessed with its position as you are with yours? Negotiating is all about making progress toward resolution and that means not being so preoccupied with your position that you fail to listen.

CHAPTER FOUR

The Offer

The first volley in the game of negotiation is the offer. Be mindful of your opening shot and ace it! Read on to see what I mean.

1. No, I Insist, You First

Not only at the outset of the negotiation, but also at every step of the way throughout the process, take as long as possible to commit to a number on your end. Once you provide a number, it's very difficult to go up or down from there. Whenever possible, it is crucial that you try your best to find a way to get the other guy to tell you what he wants first. Don't assume you know. It cannot be stressed enough how often the other party will surprise you with his first offer or request.

If you are interested in buying your neighbor's car, ask her what she would like to get for it. If you can get her to respond with a number, then you now have a starting point you won't have to go above. If you offer a number first, you may have gone much higher than her expectations!

Usually the seller of an item or the provider of a service will quote a price for his or her item or service. If you merely pay the asking price, you've obviously decided not to negotiate at all. If instead, however, you want to negotiate from that starting asking price, then you must decide whether you want to first make the seller an offer that is lower than the asking price or whether you want to try to get him or her to reduce the asking price *even before you make any offer at all.*

There are also other situations in which there is no clear starting number and, therefore, the ability to get the other party to quote a number first is a huge advantage to you. Sometimes, a seller or service provider has waited for you to make an offer for the item or service instead of providing you with the price or fee. The trading of items and the bartering of services are also examples in which no starting point has been determined. Additionally, there are times when an owner of an item or a service provider has no intentions of selling her item to you or performing a particular service for you, but you approached that person prior to her assigning a value to her item or service. Moreover, there are situations involving parties already having an existing relationship, but one party decides she now wants to receive more of something or provide less of something than before. For example, an employee may approach an employer for a raise, or a service provider may request additional fees than had previously been established between the parties. In all of these types of scenarios, the strategy of getting the other party to go first provides huge dividends for you in your negotiations.

2. Riding the Range

An enormously useful technique is to ask for a range when

the other party does not want to give you a precise number as a start of the negotiation. People often feel comfortable giving a range of numbers rather than setting one price for something. Psychologically, they feel safer, as they haven't pigeonholed themselves into a definite, precise figure. You have made them feel more comfortable and relaxed by asking for this friendly range as opposed to making them commit to a hard number. Yet, you have already tipped the negotiation heavily in your favor as their range provides the number they would accept at the lowest end and the number they would love to receive at the highest end.

If your neighbor states that she's looking for somewhere between $5,000 and $8,000 for her car, you know that means she'd be very happy if she received around $8,000, but she'd probably accept somewhere around $5,000! And, because that's really just her starting number, there's a good chance that she'd even take less than $5,000. A skilled negotiator can often convince people to accept less than they thought they'd be willing to accept at their lowest end. And you can do so while still making them feel good about the deal and about you.

To start off negotiations, you as the educated and shrewd negotiator will start with $5,000 as the number from which you begin to negotiate. Don't fall in the trap of negotiating from her high point of $8,000 when she's already told you she'd be okay with $5,000. You need to completely forget about whatever the high end of her range was—that's history. You take the lowest part of her range and immediately designate that as her asking price. The reverse is true if you're the seller and she's the buyer. If she's buying your car and states that her budget is between $5,000 and $8,000, you immediately disregard her low end and refer to $8,000 henceforth as her offer.

Let's go back to our example in which your neighbor just told you she's looking for somewhere between $5,000 and $8,000 for her car. You need to use the right words and to explain your reasoning in order to pin down $5,000 as her asking price. The quicker and more smoothly you make this transition, the better you will do with this negotiation. Your response should be, "I'm glad you gave me this range of $5,000 to $8,000, because I really like your car a lot. If you started from any number over $5,000, I know we'd be way too far off from each other to ever possibly be able to work things out. But with a starting point of $5,000, we have a good chance!" By commenting in this way, you are discarding the top of her range and honing in on only the very low end of it. Because of *how* you said it, it's now difficult for her to try to insist on anything other than her lowest end of her range, as you just made it clear that *even her low end was higher than you need it to be.*

Also note you haven't accepted her lowest end yet, and you have made it clear that even her lowest end will still have to be reduced. Now you've set the stage for her to start thinking and getting used to the concept that she's going to have to sharpen her pencil further to make a deal with you. Her reaction to your statements will indicate to you whether she's going to insist on her low point of $5,000, or whether she'll be willing to go down some from there.

If you had continued to entertain her entire range, you would never have had a chance of ending up with a final number lower than her low point of $5,000. If you had accepted her range as *the range*, at the end of the day you would have ended up stuck somewhere in the middle of $5,000 to $8,000. Your goal is to get as much of the seller's number adjusted early and quickly and be rid of the fluff. If she wasn't comfortable with an original asking price of $5,000, then she wouldn't have used that number in her range. It's important to recognize this as soon as you hear it. The rest gets easier once you've started the negotiation, correctly clearing your thoughts of any number above her low of $5,000.

Another manner by which you could have guided her to accept that her number is only $5,000 is by initially restating her $5,000 low as a hypothetical. This makes it less likely she'll resist, and makes it easier for her to go along with it. With great tact, say something like this: "Let's just say that you are at a starting point of $5,000 for a minute. Assuming that's true for now, how negotiable are you?" The trick is that you haven't made her feel too pinned down because of your careful choice in wording, but the effect is the same for your purposes.

Once she answers your question, she's essentially agreed that negotiations are starting off at $5,000. She'll most likely respond in one of two ways. She'll either respond by saying the $5,000 wouldn't be negotiable, which still means she's acknowledging and validating an asking price of $5,000. Or she'll concede that the $5,000 could be negotiable, which translates as her asking price is $5,000, eliminating the higher parts of her range, and you are probably going to be able to drop her price even more.

3. The Raphaely Turnaround

What if the people on the other side insist that you make the first offer before they make any changes to their number? You don't want to lose the "going first" battle, as you know that going first will place you at a disadvantage from the very beginning, so how do you respond? Do everything in your power to get out of it. Put up a fight. It won't always work, but it will work more often than you think. Provide a legitimate explanation as to why it makes more sense for them to start the negotiations first even if they have already provided you with their original asking price. Suppose the negotiations involve a business that you are unfamiliar with or a process more ordinarily handled by the other party. Are you hiring an editor? Are you buying your first factory from a company that specializes in the buying and selling of factories? Looking for a decorator? If it is clear that the other party has more experience than you have in this particular field, shift the pressure to start the negotiation back to him or her, explaining, "You know much more about this than I do. You are the expert on this topic."

Is the other party the seller? If so, try: "Since you own this car you know better than anyone else what you want for it, so maybe we should start by seeing what kind of range you're really looking for so I know if it's even within my budget." If the other party is the buyer, you completely flip the switch on that logic. If the buyer attempts to get you to lower your original asking price, you would now say something like, "Since you are the buyer, you know your budget better than anyone else, so maybe we should start by at least seeing what your budget is. If we're not even within range, then we won't have to waste each other's time."

Know and understand these turnaround tactics, be able to apply them to different situations, and, most of all, be able to recognize when they're being used on you. If the other side is a skilled negotiator, and you have stated, "You're the seller, so you know what you want to get for this," they may come right back at you with the same turnaround you would have used on them if the roles were reversed. They may say, "Yes, that's true, but as the buyer you should at least start by telling me your budget so we can see if you could even afford whatever price I would give you."

Anticipate this little friendly cat-and-mouse game and have a follow-up response ready. Try to shift the focus away from the budget rationale. Explain that your budget isn't important, and mention that you might be able to borrow additional money so your original budget really is of no relevance. Saying this will likely preclude you from making your budget a negotiating tactic later on, as you've now volunteered that you could come up with more money. That's okay though, because you can always turn the focus of the negotiation to the item's value and alternatives you have to buying that particular one, instead of focusing on how much you can actually afford.

It's important to understand that you make your best arguments, anticipate the other side's potential responses to your arguments, have rebuttals ready for those possible responses, and ultimately remain acutely aware as to the way every argument, response, and rebuttal you raise may limit your arsenal later in the negotiations. As you start to practice negotiating skills you become more familiar with how the dynamics of these contentions are raised, and the objections they potentially cause. Soon you will be able to weave in and out of arguments with ease, staying one step ahead at all times.

4. The Raphaely Stalling Technique

This is another clever method by which to win the "you go first" battle. Let's assume the other side is insisting that you make the first offer. You have tried to use the "Raphaely turnaround" method and they didn't budge, causing a "first offer standoff," or maybe the situation does not allow for the application of the Raphaely turnaround. You're being put on the spot to make the first offer, but you know better. If all else has failed, say something like, "I would love to make an offer and begin negotiations, but I haven't yet even thought of a number with which I'd be comfortable. I was hoping you'd be providing me with some sort of range so I could at least have a number to wrap my hands around and be able to begin to figure things out. If you insist that I come up with a number first, I'm okay with that, but I'll need some more time so I can be more prepared to do so. I will have to get back to you."

By answering in this manner, the other party sees you are willing to play ball and that you are not trying to be difficult, but pressuring you to come up with a beginning number is going to cause delays. If the people on the other side are interested in getting the ball rolling, they may succumb and drop their insistence on your making the first offer. They will be weighing the disadvantage of their having to make the first offer against their motivation to get things started. They may not wish to take the chance of losing your interest altogether if things progress too slowly. Obviously you wouldn't apply this tactic in a situation in which you know the other party is in no hurry or when you see the other party is just *not* going to make the first offer under any circumstances. If either of these conditions is present, then you may be forced to make the first offer and do your best to overcome that disadvantage later on in the negotiations.

5. Making a "Pretend" First Offer

If you must make the first offer, try to mention numbers in a manner where those numbers really are not *your* numbers. You are now merely "talking numbers." Say something like, "We aren't yet sure what we are willing to pay, but we know that the other widgets similar to this widget have been selling for ten to twenty-five dollars." You haven't committed to anything yet, but you have provided numbers, demonstrating that you are not being difficult. At the same time, you're *putting it out there* to get the other party's reaction to these numbers. It's likely that the other party will react to the numbers you just mentioned, and that reaction will provide you with clues as to what numbers he or she is thinking. Listen for what range of numbers the people on the other side try to distance themselves from and what range they try to compare themselves to. They may respond by saying something like, "Yes, that's true, but all of the ones that sold for less than $15 had only one motor and ours has two." Now you know their number is higher than $15 because they distanced their widget from those that sold for less than $15. If they believed the value of their widget was $20 or more, they would have compared their widget to ones that sold for $20. You will probably need to come up with approximately $15, or close to it, to get them to accept an offer.

6. How Low Will You *Not* Go?

A clever, quick, and easy way to find out your seller's bottom-line number without his or her even realizing you're doing so is to work backwards and find out what number he or she would *not* accept. How do you do this without having to make a very low offer yourself that might seem insulting? It's easier than you think. Toward the beginning of the negotiations—although this technique can be utilized at any time during the process—instead of throwing out a lowball offer, ask something like this: "I want to do my best to get a good deal, and I want to make you an offer, but I want to make sure I'm respectful, and I don't want to insult you. Therefore, can you please just tell me what number would insult you so I know not to say it?" Say this with all of the politeness and sincerity you can muster up.

Let's assume the seller's original asking price is $100,000. The seller may respond with something like, "I'd certainly be insulted if you offered me something ridiculous like $50,000." That is very valuable information. The seller could have said $60,000, $70,000 or any other number, but she didn't; she said $50,000. You may have been thinking of offering $50,000, but now you know better. You also know that anything substantially greater than $50,000 would not insult her and, therefore, could be considered a reasonable and potentially acceptable offer. Don't take that information and now offer $51,000, because she will probably regard that as too close to the insulting amount. But you may now feel comfortable offering $60,000, or whatever you believe is far enough off from that insulting number but nonetheless a low enough number. Anything reasonably higher than that insulting amount will at least be considered and most likely countered, thus providing you with a good starting point for negotiations.

CHAPTER FIVE

The Fundamentals

My fundamentals are a series of framing devices—ways of thinking when negotiating. If you master the following practices, you will be ahead every step of the way. When you are in the thick of negotiation, it takes discipline to stay focused on what matters. The techniques in this chapter will ensure that you close your deal successfully.

1. Working the Baseline

Get in the habit of *always* wondering whether you can get the other parties to sweeten the deal. If they have made some adjustments or concessions, don't assume they won't continue to make more of them. The only way you can find out how much the other side is willing to give up is by continuing to ask. Naturally, you'll need to know when to stop, but learn to be comfortable with asking if this is the absolute best they can do. Always be on the lookout for additional reasons to gain further concessions from them. Has there been a misunderstanding that, upon clarification, ultimately makes the deal less desirable for you? Have you received other offers while these negotiations are still taking place? Have you become aware of anything about the other party that could provide you with reason for apprehension or doubt? Assuming you are still comfortable dealing with them, refer to any of these factors as justification for further concessions or adjustments.

If you sense that your position is strong and they are motivated to close this deal, merely demonstrating hesitation to get the deal finalized could cause them to offer more concessions. If you believe they could afford to make the deal a little sweeter, try saying: "I really want to conclude this deal, but I just don't know. I'm excited about getting this done, and yet when I take a step back and think about things I start feeling like I'm not getting enough (or I'm giving up too much). I'm trying my best to get over that feeling." Notice how you haven't made any more demands, and you haven't asked the other party to change anything. You are simply demonstrating some apprehension in the hope of a deal-sweetener to entice you to finalize the discussions. They can respond by saying they cannot make any additional changes, or they may respond with an improved offer.

As long as you are nice and respectful, this hesitation shouldn't create any hard feelings from the other side. Essentially, you have nothing to lose by saying this. But you must do a good job of assessing their reactions leading up to this so that you know when to stop asking for changes; otherwise, at some point you do run the risk that the other side no longer takes you seriously and possibly becomes annoyed.

2. Enter Swinging the Ax

At every step of the process, chop down at the price when

negotiating to purchase something. Use *every* meeting, phone call, or discussion with the other party throughout the course of the negotiation to continue to try to get a better deal. You will do much better with your negotiations if you get the price down in phases. Each time you speak with the other party is a fresh opportunity to ask questions in different ways and employ the various negotiating tools you possess as a skilled negotiator.

If negotiations will be taking place in person, always start your negotiations *before* you even see the item the other person is selling or before you meet the person with whom you will be negotiating. If you see an asking price of $10,000 for an antique armoire, you must start chopping down at that price *before you meet the seller or see the armoire.* That is an integral part of the "chopping down process." In person, it would usually be much more difficult to get the other side to go down from $10,000 to $7,500 at one time. But what if you were able to get her down to $9,000 even before you saw the armoire? Now you would already have $1,000 of the difference covered before you even meet!

People usually feel uncomfortable getting into details about the numbers until after the first conversation, believing that the first contact with the seller should be reserved for small talk, asking for directions and getting preliminary information about the item itself. Wrong! The initial contact is a golden opportunity—not to be wasted—to begin to make a dent in the price. Sellers often make the same mistake. Why not inquire of a potential buyer if your asking price is within the buyer's budget? As the seller, you establish legitimacy for your asking price at the outset and weed out potential buyers looking to chop down hard at your price.

Begin your fact-finding mission as soon as you begin communications with a seller. Within the first couple of minutes after getting into the details of the deal, one of your first questions should be something to the effect of, "I know your asking price is ten thousand dollars, but what is the lowest amount you would take for this armoire?" The seller will probably give you a lower number than the original asking price right then, as everyone feels a sense of obligation to reduce their price somewhat from an original asking price when asked to do so. Take full advantage of that easy first step.

Every time you get to a lower price, you must completely forget—and make the other party completely forget—the original asking price, or the price the seller had been asking for before he or she agreed to the new number. If the original asking price was $100,000, and you've successfully chopped that down to $90,000 in the beginning of negotiations, don't allow the original $100,000 asking price to be brought up again. You are now negotiating from $90,000, not $100,000. Likewise, if you're able to continue to reduce the seller's number lower than $90,000, then negotiations are based on that new number, and the fact that the seller's number was once $90,000 is history, never to be referred to again.

3. Dismiss Reminders of the Original Price

Let's assume the seller's original asking price was $500, but you were able to get him to reduce his price down to $450, and then again to $400, and now his revised asking price is down to $375. As negotiations continue, he will want to remind you as to how much he has already conceded in lowering his asking price. He may say things like, "I've already made huge sacrifices." Downplay his concessions by saying, "I agree you've come down a lot, but please realize that your number was way too high to begin with. I'm glad I was optimistic and willing to stick it out because now we're really getting close."

4. Don't Bid Against Yourself

In a negotiation, it is always a good idea to get at least one offer from the other side in between your offers. If you ask for $50 and the buyer offers you $20, it's fair that the ball is now in your court to come up with the next number. If you now say $40, you want her to come back with a number until this process repeats enough for the two of you to agree. What you absolutely don't want is for you to have said $40 and then for her to respond that it's still too high and that she isn't prepared to go above $20. If she insists on staying at her number, you'll be tempted to come down from your $40 to $30 so she becomes more likely to budge some more. Try your best not to do it, because if you do, then you've essentially just bid against yourself and just earned her an easy $10 while setting the stage for her to continue to take advantage of this. She may now offer $22 or $23, knowing you'll likely continue to make bigger adjustments than her most recent adjustment of $2 or $3. The likely result will probably be some number closer to $20 than $30. If you had insisted that she go up from $20 when it was her turn to make a counteroffer before you went down to $30, you'd be in a much better position as the two of you continued with the negotiations.

If you see you're dealing with a skilled negotiator who's attempting to get you to bid against yourself in this manner because she's refusing to counter and essentially forcing you to provide two numbers in a row, then you should ask her to "give me some number so I don't feel like I'm bidding against myself." Most people will respect this request and at least provide some number, even if it's not a big jump. Any change is still better than you having to come up with two numbers in a row.

5. Get the Other Side to Bid Against Themselves

Always do your best to get the other guy to bid against himself. Whenever possible, stay put at your number and see whether you can get him to provide two numbers in a row. Anytime you can do this you're winning the negotiation. Often you'll recognize other people committing this huge mistake without even realizing it. If you find yourself dealing with such novice negotiators, certainly don't draw it to their attention, and make no reference to "bidding against oneself" because once you point it out they'll be aware and sensitized about this issue.

At the very outset, after you display disappointment in their first offer, let that sink in for a little while before you start providing your own numbers. Let them get on the defensive about their offer, and see how they react. They may have already expected that their number would be rejected and thrown the number out there in the hopes that you were going to be an easy target. Seeing that you're not rushing to accept their original terms, they may follow up with adjustments or concessions. Feel them out for as long as you can before you rush to verbalize any numbers of your own.

Let's assume your neighbor just offered you $500 for your sofa and that you were hoping to receive a higher offer. Instead of rejecting the buyer's offer or making a counteroffer, just say, "I was looking to get more than $500." Next, talk about how great your sofa is, how expensive it was when you bought it brand-new, or how unique it is with its custom fabric or unusual feather fill. Let the buyer see your disappointment in her offer. She may surprise you. You may have been tempted to ask for $550. Instead, your delay provides the opportunity for your neighbor to suggest another number of her own, essentially bidding against herself. She may now offer $600, which you would have never received if you had made a counteroffer of $550 too soon.

You will win your negotiations if you can learn how to get the other parties to provide their numbers while you focus on your responses to their numbers. Let's say you are the seller. If they start at twenty dollars, keep the focus on them and on their thought process instead of responding with a number of your own. Say something like, "Well, that's much lower than I was hoping for. I was hoping we'd at least be pretty close to each other's numbers. It looks like we have a long way to go." Then you can remain silent and see if they say anything. Again, the more turns they take in between your turns, the better you'll do. If the silent pause doesn't work, then turn it around on them and say something like, "Can you make me a higher offer so at least I can feel like we have a chance of working something out here?"

A good rule of thumb is to try to get them to go twice in a row before you go once. If you try to get them to make three adjustments to your every one they may become agitated. But, getting them to adjust twice to your every one may not even be noticeable to them. So, in this example, if they then come back with a revised offer of twenty-five dollars, you could then respond with a number of your own. When they provide a number (or any relevant terms), *hold the focus on them again*: Can they do better? Explain why the number offered won't work, why you have other options, or why they should be more open-minded.

Although you are paying close attention to how many times in a row each of you is making adjustments, the unskilled negotiator has so many thoughts and ideas running through his or her head that key tactics such as this one are overlooked. In fact, you've probably fallen victim to this tactic at least once in the past without even realizing it!

6. Keep Some Chips in Your Pocket!

If you initially set their expectations low, the people on the other side will end up feeling like they received more than they would have if you had set their expectations higher at the outset. Don't begin with an insulting number, but start as far away from your *actual* number as you can without appearing unreasonable. As you negotiate—from their perspective—any concession or adjustment you make now seems like a greater gain. They will end up happy, feeling like they bargained well.

Once you have to commit to some number, make sure it's much lower than what you're really willing to pay if you are buying and much higher than you're really willing to accept if you are selling. Remember, negotiations usually take place in stages or phases, involving give and take, which leads each party to feel like he made sacrifices. Each party wants to feel like he "got a good deal," like the other side gave in on price or other terms and that he wasn't the only one who got less than he asked for. That's human nature, a key factor in almost every negotiation.

Let's assume you're interested in buying a hair salon business that is for sale. You know the asking price is $200,000, and the seller wants to have the buyer take over all operations and expenses within the next ninety days. Also, the seller plans on taking her best employee and fifteen thousand dollars' worth of hair-care products with her to the new shop she's opening two towns away. Additionally, the seller is looking to get paid at least 50 percent of her asking price in cash up front, with the remaining 50 percent paid in monthly payments over several years. As you can see, there are many terms involved in this deal in its entirety. All of this is aside from issues that will arise throughout the process that have not even yet been thought of or addressed.

Let's assume further that you are only willing to pay $180,000 for the business and that you need to have 120 days before you will be ready to take over the operations and expenses. Also, you're okay with her taking her best employee and the fifteen thousand dollars' worth of products, and that you are prepared to put down 50 percent of the price. Your "up-front" money is only 50 percent of $180,000, which is $90,000, and not 50 percent of the $200,000 the seller is requesting, which would have been $100,000 in up-front money.

If you start off by offering $180,000, you're offering her $20,000 less than she wants. She's already not going to be happy because of the price reduction, so you're certainly not in a great position to be asking for an additional thirty days or for changes to her up-front money request. You've left yourself with no wiggle room. Instead, begin by offering $160,000, which she probably rejects. The difference now, however, is that you know you have an additional $20,000 to work with, "chips in your pocket" for later. After she rejects your initial offer of $160,000, try to get her to provide a counteroffer. Assuming she does, it's still likely to be close to her original asking price of $200,000.

You now can raise your initial offer from $160,000 to a higher amount, but in exchange for this increase, insist on her being more flexible regarding some of the other terms of the deal. Your wiggle room has earned you some concessions because you've made it appear that anything over $160,000 is out of your comfort zone. She has to give up something in return for your raising the offer from $160,000 to $180,000. Had you originally offered $180,000, she would have rejected the offer. But now, because you've made a substantial improvement to your original offer, you've placed yourself in a better position to negotiate on the other terms that are still crucial to you in this deal, such as the amount of up-front money and the time you have to take over the business.

7. How to Bid Low Without Being Insulting

It is possible to go very low without being insulting. As with everything else, it's all in what you say and how you say it. Let's assume you finally have to give your number, but you know that your number is going to be way too low and could possibly insult or even anger the other party. Start by educating yourself on the seller's number and how it was arrived at. Accordingly, you have to come in with a number low enough so that the seller's counter would still allow you to be in your desired range. The key to the very low offer technique is to come up with a good excuse as to why your number is low.

Don't attack the seller or the product; rather, make it clear you understand that it's a low offer, but you have sincere, legitimate reasons for making it anyway. The reason could be that you completely underestimated the item's cost when you worked out your budget for it, but you're hoping the seller doesn't want to have to negotiate with any more people. You might say you have less money available than you thought, but you're hoping somehow something can still be worked out. You could say you recognize your offer is low but you'd be very appreciative if they would still consider it.

Whatever you say, the point is to keep your number low while being apologetic. If you are the first to admit your offer is low then you take away their reason to be angry. They won't be as likely to assume you're trying to take advantage of them and more likely to consider your bid. They may counter with something reasonable rather than cutting off communications. Don't forget that negotiations involve a great amount of psychology.

Present a good reason for why every single dollar matters to you now. This will excuse your meager financial position. For example, if you're looking at buying a truck, you could point out you only have a certain amount of money to spend and that you also have to consider the fact that you will have to buy snow tires right away. Or you could demonstrate to them how much gas money you have to budget for because this truck won't get the same mileage as the other vehicles you're considering. Or maybe you can bring up how much more expensive the insurance on this sports car is in comparison with the other cars you're considering. This way, it's clear to the other party that you have other immediate expenses associated with this purchase.

On the one hand, it's not cool to "make your problems their problems." Why should they care what else you have to spend your money on or what else you need? On the other hand, however, it doesn't hurt for them to understand and appreciate the total amount of money you'll have to spend all at one time, even if it's not all going to them.

8. Get an Answer Early in the Process

You'd be surprised how many people will come close to literally telling you their actual bottom-line number, if you simply ask them. Therefore, don't be afraid to ask, and ask early in the process. Notice that "how much do you absolutely need to get?" is much different from "what is your asking price?" or "how much do you want?" You have taken the focus away from wants and brought it down to just needs. Everyone wants to get top dollar, but what does a seller actually *have to be* offered in order to say yes? For example, the seller may want to get as much as his neighbors got for their house, but he may actually only need to get enough to pay off his existing mortgage.

You say something like, "I know your original asking price is one hundred thousand dollars, but have you thought about what you absolutely *need to get* to really make a deal? Is there some threshold amount you know you absolutely *must get* to make it work for you?" Most people, when asked in this manner, will lower their asking price. What a simple way for you to get them to reduce their price quickly and easily without even having made an offer of your own!

9. Always Ask About Other Offers

A question about other offers the seller has received need not sound intrusive. You are being curious, just doing your best to get all the facts. When you ask, "Have you had any other offers?" you are likely to get some very valuable information. For example, the response could be, "Yes, I have received two offers of fifty dollars each, but I didn't accept them."

Your follow-up question should be: "Do you mind telling me why you didn't accept those offers?" Don't assume anything. You can ask more questions about those offers. Were they offers in installments? Were the buyers going to pick it up in four weeks? If so, maybe the seller would take fifty dollars, but maybe he didn't want to store the item, or wait weeks for the money. Perhaps he now says "Fifty dollars is just way too low. I may have been okay with seventy-five."

It could be that you have just heard his real, desired number simply because you asked about other offers. Additionally, if he answered some of your other follow-up questions, you may now also know more about his goals regarding time frame and any other terms about which he's concerned. If he responds that asking him about other offers is intrusive, simply apologize and say something like, "I ask too many questions sometimes" or "Sorry, I was just curious." As long as you show you are apologetic, it should not damage the relationship. Only in rare instances will this questioning hurt your negotiations, so it is usually worth taking the shot if you bounce back nicely should the seller get upset.

10. Don't Insult the Merchandise

Remember that people take pride in their possessions. You are certainly entitled to point out major defects, but keep in mind that people take criticism of their belongings personally. Can you remember back to a time when you were selling something? Did a shopper just go on and on about what it was missing, what was broken, or what needed to be replaced? Did you feel insulted, and did you dislike them and not want to give in to them? Unskilled negotiators make those mistakes. You want the seller to like you.

For example, don't say things like, "There seems to be a lot of wear and tear on this car. It looks pretty dented up." Instead, shift your focus, saying, "I've got to say your car looks great, but I just need to point out to you that similar cars I've looked at were literally in near perfect, mint condition. It's okay, because your car is very nice, but I just hope we can figure that into the final price we negotiate."

In this manner, you still made your point, but you did so in a milder and less insulting way. Point out defects gently. "Can we work out some discount for the dent on the passenger door? Have you looked into how much it would cost to get that fixed? The car will look perfect once that gets fixed." This way without being offensive you are still managing to bring up the dent and the fact that you expect the final price to reflect it.

11. Never Accept Any Offer Too Quickly

Even if you've just heard the offer of your dreams, appear to pause and weigh your options in your head. If you accept an offer too quickly, the people on the other side will be convinced they could have done better and you would have been happy with a lower offer. They might try to change things, back out, or get some additional after-the-fact concessions from you. It's simply human nature.

All of a sudden, at the eleventh hour, they may try to change a part of the deal, saying something like, "You are shipping the car to me, right?" They may even start making it appear as if they understood some of the terms of the deal differently than you did.

Another potential risk of accepting an offer too enthusiastically is that the other side may begin to distrust the item or service. Is something wrong with this item, if you are so quick to accept their offer? You always want your counterparts to feel like they got a good deal, so watch out for overeagerness!

12. How to React

No matter what, you need to act somewhat disappointed when you receive an offer or asking price. Don't question the person's fairness and don't be insulting; instead, act surprised and make it seem like you weren't expecting that number because you weren't prepared to pay that much or accept that little. You were hoping for and expecting better. Remember, most of the time individuals or companies don't start with their best rock-bottom price. If you don't question it at all, you won't get any adjustments.

When they provide you with their offer, they will be doing their best to read your reaction by watching your expressions and other nonverbal cues and by listening carefully to what you say and how you say it. They will rely on their assessment during the remainder of the negotiation. You must handle this critical point with the skill and care necessary to set the tone for the entire process. By showing them that you are disappointed and expecting something better, you lose nothing. You will still have the opportunity to accept their offer if it was originally acceptable to you. They are not going to take away their offer because you hesitated at first. In fact, it's more likely that they'd take away their offer if you demonstrate you're too eager to accept it.

Ask them to justify their position and try to convince you that their offer is fair. The more convincing they need to do, the more satisfied they'll be when you ultimately "are convinced."

Let's assume you're selling your house. You list it for $100,000, but you would realistically accept $85,000, and you are selling your house yourself and not through a realtor. You receive an offer of $85,000—which you are tempted to accept. But you remember: appear to be slightly disappointed (while polite and friendly) so your body language, facial expressions, and tone of voice communicate that you were hoping to receive a higher offer. You say something like, "That is a lower offer than we expected. I'm hoping that's just your starting point to negotiate and that you can adjust that number."

As a result, the buyers will make an adjustment or concession, justify their position but remain firm, or remain firm without justifying their position. If they make an adjustment or concession, you just earned yourself a better deal because you displayed disappointment, although in reality you would have been happy to accept their original $85,000 offer. If they make no adjustments or concessions, but at least work at justifying their offer to you, then your acceptance of their offer is a concession made by you. As a result, they will feel better about the deal than if you had immediately demonstrated satisfaction with their offer. Consequently, it will be easier for you to get a concession on the many other issues that will arise later before the deal is completely executed.

Keep in mind that little things always seem to come up even after all parties believe they have covered all issues. It's always good to have your counterparts feel like they "owe you one" rather than the other way around. In sum, it almost never hurts to demonstrate some disappointment with their original asking price or offer.

Along the same lines, and for the same reasons, it's recommended that you also downplay any satisfaction with the final results of a negotiation. As with your initial reaction to an offer, if you make it obvious that you got exactly what you wanted, the other party is going to feel remorse, or feel that they could have gotten more from you. Accordingly, they may then look for ways to avoid fulfilling their obligations in accordance with the terms of the deal.

13. The Raphaely Takeaway

You have to be willing to bluff. Sometimes you need to show that you are willing to walk away. You have nothing to lose because there are many ways by which you can "come back" after a failed bluff attempt. Knowing this should provide you with the confidence to bluff when you have to. People become more thankful for the deal you presented them after it has seemingly been taken away from them.

Make sure not to make it personal and not to say anything insulting, because one wrong remark at this time could be all it takes to prevent them from reaching back out to you later. Never express your bluff in permanent and absolute terms. Instead, make it clear that you are hoping to hear from them again. Make it easy for them to save face in the event they change their minds and want to reach out to you later.

Say something like, "It just doesn't look like we're going to be able to work anything out. It was a pleasure working on this deal with you, and I'm very sorry we couldn't make it happen. I'm still hoping you will change your mind about the price and call me with good news."

After you inform them that you are walking away, be silent and listen to what the other side says and closely observe how they react. If they do or say anything that indicates they still want to work things out now, you have just significantly strengthened your position. If, on the other hand, they seem to be okay with it not working out, keep in mind they may be doing some bluffing of their own at this point. Now you have to assess your next options, based on the circumstances and on how things have gone until this point. Do you walk away for now and see what transpires over the next couple of days? Do you walk away for good? Or do you "undo" your bluff immediately? Those decisions will be based on your immediate, realistic assessment of how far off you are from your goals and how badly you want to make this deal. If you now find yourself uncomfortable with walking away, then start to undo your bluff immediately.

14. How to Handle a Failed Bluff

To undo a bluff immediately, speak up quickly before the conversation or meeting is over. This is easier than you think. Put your pride and ego aside, and get the job done. Take a pause. Then demonstrate that you are upset that the two of you couldn't come to terms after all the effort each party put into working it out. Point out that you like them, you've enjoyed trying to work things out with them, and you feel a sense of sadness for not being able to come together. Next, tell them you don't want to have to go through this again with someone new.

You're *not* making it about the fact that you can't live without this deal; instead, you're making it about the fact that the two of you have worked so hard and come so far that it's a shame not to see the deal through to its completion. Create the image of someone who doesn't like to fail or give up. You feel a connection with this person and want to succeed together on solving the remaining problems. When you speak in these terms, you aren't undoing your bluff from a position of weakness.

If you believe you don't have to undo your bluff immediately, wait to see if they contact you at some point. If they don't contact you, then you might call them saying the same types of things you would have said in the event of an immediate "undo." You could say: "I've been thinking about things, and I've concluded that I gave up on this too quickly. I know you are a reasonable person, and I shouldn't have assumed that we wouldn't be able to work things out."

Note that at no time are you saying that you're agreeing to give them exactly what they wanted. You are just suggesting that negotiations be opened again. You aren't giving in yet, and maybe enough time has passed which has made them realize they are now willing to offer an additional adjustment. You are still—and always—negotiating, even after undoing your bluff. You are committed to opening discussions again, if they are willing.

Another route is to ask your spouse, friend, business partner, or other designated person to reach out to the other side on your behalf, saying something like, "I am reaching out to you on Mike's behalf because I know he's being stubborn, but he truly wants to work this out with you. Maybe you can help me get you guys back on track. Can you make a concession or counter his last offer so he can accept and go forward with the deal?" Remember, you use this tactic when you are already reasonably convinced that you have nothing to lose at this point, as your bluff didn't work.

15. Recognize When You Need to Encourage the Other Side

What do you do if you sincerely want to work out a deal with the other side, but you sense they're getting frustrated that things aren't moving along more quickly or easily? Take a break away from the actual process and do your best to point out to them how much ground you have already covered. You could say, "I know we are still five thousand dollars away from each other in our negotiations, but what a difference this is from where we began—at twenty thousand dollars apart!"

Obviously, you don't want to appear desperate or overeager, but you do want to reassure them that you've traveled a long distance together and that soon you will be in agreement. Simply by demonstrating that you are confident that the deal will work out will encourage your counterparts to feel the same way.

16. Think Outside the Box

What do you do if you've exhausted all imaginable possibilities and negotiations have come to a standstill? Then it's time to be creative. You need to have in mind mutually acceptable and fair methods by which to resolve any remaining differences. Is there another person you both trust who could step in to help work out the remaining issues? Or how about introducing unrelated items into the negotiation to make up for any remaining disparity?

Let's assume both parties are still one thousand dollars apart on the price of the bedroom set you want to buy. Maybe you happen to have four theater tickets to an upcoming show and you already know you won't be able to make it. You could suggest that you throw in the tickets to close the gap in your deal. You never know until you try!

You could try a little personal service barter. What do you do for a living or as a hobby? Are you a caterer or an interior decorator or good at training a dog? Is there a service you can offer that would be worth $600 to the buyer? If so, maybe you could narrow the gap down to a remaining $400 difference? Now you only have to come up with $400 more out of your pocket. Learn to think outside the box when you are boxed in.

17. Answer Questions with Questions

Don't frustrate the other side, but use every opportunity you can to get more information and additional insight. Each time you share a fact about yourself, make sure to learn something new in return. Sometimes it can be very helpful to find out the reasoning behind a question that was posed to you. If you assume you know the logic behind your counterpart's questions, you may be missing excellent opportunities to bring up helpful follow-up points.

18. Ask Why

You will gain valuable insight from the other side if you can get in the habit of asking why. With "why?" you are basically saying, "Give me more information about that." If you are told the seller needs to get $50,000 for a piece of land, don't make the mistake of accepting that number as the beginning of the negotiation process. First, ask why this amount is needed. Is $50,000 the amount owed on it? If so, did the seller overpay when she bought it? Did she miss payments, thereby causing her balance to be higher than it really should be? Is she essentially making her problems your problems?

Having done your research, you may learn that the seller needs to get $50,000 because she envisioned netting $10,000 after paying off her loan of $40,000. Or (if she's selling her old luxury car) maybe she is looking to buy a replacement that will cost her $50,000, and the replacement is newer with more features. If so, you can point out to her that the asking price is obviously too high if there is another one being sold for the same price that is both newer and "loaded."

The benefits of asking why hold true for any type of negotiation. If your employee requests a 20 percent raise, ask why he thinks he deserves a 20 percent raise. How did he arrive at 20 percent? Do you agree with his assessment or do you have objections to the points he raised that would demonstrate to him that 20 percent is too much?

If someone offers you $100 for your widget even though your asking price was $200, ask them why they're only offering you $100. Is that all they can afford? If so, you can let them pay you the rest at a later time. Have they seen other widgets just like yours selling for only $100? Have they underestimated or misunderstood some of the features of your widget? Whatever their reason is will be useful information as you negotiate with them.

19. Freebies

Are there things you can "throw in" to the deal that don't matter much to you but that could allow the other person to save face? Can you concede on any of those terms in exchange for getting what you want on another point that is more important to you? Can you offer something in addition to the terms that have already been covered that could sweeten the deal?

Maybe you're selling a car out of your used-car lot. Do you also have a repair shop adjacent to your lot? What if you threw in free oil changes for five years? Your buyer may calculate that those free oil changes will save him or her a total of $600 or more over those five years. You've calculated that those oil changes will actually only cost you approximately one hundred dollars and could ultimately lead to more business for your repair shop, if your mechanic happens to find other things that need to be repaired while performing the oil changes.

Maybe you're an individual selling your own car. You know you have an extra set of snow tires for this car you were going to try to sell separately. As you think about it, however, you recognize that you'll never find the time to sell them, and that those snow tires will just end up occupying valuable space in your garage. You haven't mentioned the snow tires, but now you've reached the crunch time of the negotiation, as you and the buyer are $250 apart. Is it realistic to think that the snow tires are worth approximately $400? Tell the buyer about the snow tires, that you were hoping to sell them separately for around $400, but that maybe the two of you can work out a deal that includes the snow tires. Maybe you could throw in the tires for free to work out the remaining $250 difference.

Maybe you own a shipping company. Your company is very efficient and can ship a potential client's products in half the time it would take any other shipping company at no additional cost. Instead of just randomly blurting out that your company will get the client's shipment completed faster than other companies, why not say something like, "If we agree to ship your products in fifteen days rather than the standard thirty days, will you agree to pay two dollars per mile instead of the one dollar per mile you've been proposing?" You've thrown in something you'd be providing anyway, but now you are getting something in return!

20. One Last Chop

Negotiate a great deal, raise all of your important points, utilize all of your negotiation tactics, but save a nice rationale for a final price adjustment for the very end—what I call the "last chop." At some point, based on many factors, including what the buyers can afford, they will come up with their final offer. Now you present some other reason—a new point—for which they might be willing to adjust their offer again. At the end of the day, if someone wants to make a deal with you, there's almost always at least a little bit of cushion left over.

Let's assume you're negotiating with a software company to develop software for your business. You've agreed to final pricing, but you want to give the old ax one last swing and see if there's anything left to chop. Say something like, "This deal is great, and we're so close to signing on. We still just wish there was some way in which you could drop the final price by one percent so we have enough money left over to buy that new server we are now going to need. We know you're giving us a great deal, but what if we agreed to place your logo on our website, link to your website from there and even write something on our home page about how great you guys are?" They need to believe that you are so close to making the deal that this final little discount will definitely make it happen.

You aren't backing out of the deal you have thus far. Instead, you are proposing what could be a very nice, mutually beneficial exchange in which they further discount their pricing and you essentially help them with advertising. Had you suggested or offered to do this in the very beginning, that factor would have already been considered earlier along with all of the other factors they considered when they determined the best price they could provide and this last opportunity would have been lost.

21. Verbal Cues

Certain phrases like "we are looking for," "we are asking," and "would you consider," demonstrate an obvious willingness to negotiate. Of course, if the other side hasn't used this kind of language, you should still generally assume everything is negotiable to a certain extent. Listen carefully for the go-ahead language that signals you to get more aggressive with your side of the negotiation.

22. Careful with Those Increments

You risk the possibility of hurting your credibility if you go up or down in increments that seem rather large. For instance, if you ask for one hundred thousand dollars and then immediately go down to fifty thousand dollars, the other party will not trust you, will think something is wrong with what you're offering, or will not take you seriously. Even if you are ultimately prepared to go down that much, do so in stages that seem more credible. Additionally, keep in mind that if you use large increments, the other side will come to expect these and, when the large adjustments cease, the negotiations could come to an abrupt standstill because smaller increments will appear too trivial in comparison.

23. Make a Mountain Out of a Molehill

Ask for concessions you don't really care about and know you probably won't be granted. Then pretend you are disappointed when you don't get these breaks. It will make it easier for you to deny some of their requests, and smooth the way as you push harder for the concessions you truly care about.

Let's assume you are negotiating with a vendor. Before this meeting, while doing your research you learned that this vendor is behind on his projects and, as a result, he is going to take two weeks longer than his competitors would need to deliver the finished product. You also know that he is aware that his turn times are currently much slower than the competition. Lastly, let's assume you don't care about the additional two weeks because you are not in a hurry. As you are negotiating price and other relevant terms, ask him about a completion and delivery date.

He tells you it would take two months, that he is sorry about this long delay, but that there is absolutely nothing he can do about it. The unskilled negotiator says something like, "Well, that's okay because we don't really need it until autumn."

Handling the situation in this manner is a terrible waste of a good opportunity. Make a mountain out of a molehill! You should say: "I like working with your company, but that's a problem. The other companies we've spoken with would get this done two weeks faster than you." See how he reacts. He could potentially surprise you by letting you know he can move things around and deliver two weeks earlier like his competitors could. That's not good for you, because you'd rather have him feeling like he owes you than actually get the product on time. But you are prepared and have anticipated all possible permutations. So, if he responds in that manner, you say something like: "No, that's okay, I don't want you to have to make special accommodations for me, and I don't want someone else's delivery to be delayed because of me. Is there anything you could do on price to make up for the extra wait?"

Or maybe you're at the car dealership looking to buy a car, but the dealership only has the car you want in silver. That's really the color you prefer, but you certainly don't need to let the dealership know that. Instead, you could make an issue of the fact that the dealership has no other color choices to offer you. This would be even better if you can inform your salesperson that his or her competitor ten minutes away has this same car in silver, black and white, and that black is actually the color you want. If your salesperson suggests he or she could work out a deal with the other dealership and get the exact car you want, of course you'd respond by telling him or her that makes no sense to you, because you might as well just go to the other dealership yourself. Instead, just continue to remind your salesperson, without overdoing it, that this car is really not the ideal choice for you because of the color. This is putting the dealership on notice that it will have to be more aggressive with its pricing to earn your business.

Essentially, you want to discover what choice, feature, or option is *unavailable* on the item or service for which you are negotiating, and then you want to make it seem like you're disappointed that choice, feature, or option is unavailable. Demonstrate that you are giving up something that is important to you if you work out a deal with them. Accordingly, it's implied that you're expecting a better deal than you'd be receiving elsewhere because here you can't get your first choice. What option do they have but to knock down their price?

24. Build Your Side of the Negotiation

Use all information received to guide your follow-up questions so that you constantly refine the specifics of the transaction. If the seller mentions something about the car being painted at some point in the past, make sure you don't just go on to the next topic of discussion. Ask why the car was painted. When the seller informs you the car was scraped by a shopping cart in a grocery store parking lot, don't stop asking questions.

Make sure not to seem to be interrogating or questioning the seller's credibility. Manage your inquiries, body language, and tone so that it appears that you are simply curious by nature. You could say, "It's terrible that you had to deal with that kind of stuff. Did you ever find out how it happened? Did you ever get anyone to pay for it?" Your next questions could provide you with additional information, as you essentially are still making sure you're getting the complete story.

Obviously, you're trying to determine whether the car was really painted because it had been in a serious accident, as that could potentially reduce the value of the car. As you are appearing just to be a curious person, you could ask, "At what grocery store did this take place? I must make sure not to park the car there!" Listen carefully to the response—is the seller able to answer without any apparent hesitation? Or does it seem that you are not hearing the true story?

Assume you are an employer conducting an interview. If

the candidate you're interviewing tells you he or she resigned from a past position, ask plenty of follow-up questions so that you can gain helpful insight into what really took place. If the candidate tells you he or she resigned because the company had lost business and no longer seemed like a good opportunity, you could ask, "Did you speak with your boss before you resigned to try to determine whether they were fixing the issues? Did other people feel the same way you did? Did they resign as well, or did they stay? Do you know how that company is doing now? Has their business picked up?" The answers to these follow-up questions will provide you with a better sense of what really took place, and they may potentially lead you to information about what kind of person you're dealing with and whether he or she is being completely truthful. This will prove useful to you as you decide whether to hire this person and negotiate his or her compensation.

25. Roll with the Punches

If the other person points out reasons why you should adjust the price or any of the terms, you should be ready to demonstrate that you had already taken that particular point into consideration when you originally determined your price. For example, the other person may point out a dent on the passenger door of the car you're selling. You could reply, "Yes, I'm aware of the dent, and that's why I had originally priced the car at $5,000 instead of $5,500." It is difficult for the buyer to argue with that logic. The market will determine whether your price is fair, but if you respond confidently, your buyer might possibly conclude that the price has indeed already been adjusted to account for the dent.

26. The Fake Counteroffer

Let's assume you're asking for $5,000 for your Persian rug. The other side offers $4,500, which you would gladly accept. In reality, you would have accepted $4,000. Even so, you must counter the offer rather than accept it at first. If you accept the $4,500 without countering, the buyer is going to feel like she got a bad deal and should have offered less. Counter with something reasonable like $4,750. Later, you can agree to accept her offer of $4,500. She'll end up feeling like she got a better deal. The more you make her work through the negotiation without overdoing it or being unreasonable, the more she'll appreciate the fruits of her labor.

27. Ask General Questions

Be careful not to reveal what the "right" answer would be as part of your question. For instance, if you are buying a used car and you want to find out how often the oil was changed, don't ask whether the oil was changed every three thousand miles. The question itself makes it fairly clear that it's important to you that the oil was changed that often. Of course, the seller will reply in the affirmative. Instead, ask general questions such as, "What kind of maintenance has been done on the car?" You could even ask whether the oil had been changed, but don't telegraph any specifics about the answer you want to hear.

28. Ask "What If" Questions

Asking a "what if" question is a quick and easy way by which to find out how willing the other party may be to adjust his or her terms. Would your counterpart make an adjustment if you change some part of the equation? Think: What if I picked it up right now? What if we delivered it tomorrow? What if we throw in an extra widget? What if I were to buy an extra widget? What if I recommend your services to my friends and get you additional business? What if I buy the car that has more miles than this one? What if I buy the car that has been on your lot longer than this one? What if we let you rent back the house from us for a year so that you will have more time to find the perfect replacement house? What if we add an early termination clause in this contract so that you could get out of this contract early without being in breach? You are being creative, which may open the door for more potential solutions, while also providing yourself with a useful way to obtain more information from your counterparts when they respond to your "what if" suggestions.

29. Pay Me Now or Pay Me Later

When negotiating prices or costs, it's helpful to understand that the numbers can be seen from a cash-flow perspective or from an absolute-cost perspective. As a buyer, your objectives should always be both issues. Before you start a negotiation, you want to know when to apply each perspective and how each way of looking at the numbers affects the negotiation. Always be ready to speak in terms of cash flow *or* total cost when shifting the focus can benefit you. Additionally, always be ready for the other party to shift the focus to their benefit. Be on the lookout for the shift, know when to anticipate it, and have your responses ready to address it.

Let's assume you're interested in buying expensive software for your company. The total cost for the software is one hundred thousand dollars, but you're still working on negotiating that cost down. The software vendor may anticipate that the high cost could present a cash-flow situation and therefore may suggest a lease or payment plan. You now can't use your cash-flow issue to negotiate the price down because the vendor has now alleviated any concerns regarding cash flow.

To maintain your credibility and ensure that you are ready for a possible shift to a concession on cash flow, make it clear that *total price* is an issue *as well* from the outset. Accordingly, to cover all of your bases, you should open negotiations by stating, "We have several issues with this price of one hundred thousand dollars. First of all, we will need to figure out how we can get the total price down. We have been able to maintain a successful company because we always do our best to get a good deal on everything we purchase. I know it may be possible for you to offer us a lease option or payment plan, and we're happy to explore that and hope to be able to get our payments down as low as possible for our monthly cash-flow purposes, but we also need to be careful with the total cost."

Vendors are very experienced and skilled with presenting costs and expenses to their customers in terms of monthly payments or some other breakdown of costs so that the customer loses sight of the total amount of money he or she is spending. Car dealerships, office-machinery companies, and other sellers of big-ticket items love to negotiate with you in terms of monthly payment. Don't let them do that until you have negotiated the total price first. It's tempting to let them throw in extra costs and features when you are looking at the expenses in terms of "only an extra $250 per month," but you must realize that $250 per month amounts to $30,000, if you're making monthly payments for ten years.

Mortgage loan officers have also perfected this skill. Craftily, they include their fees into the total amount of your mortgage. When you are borrowing $300,000 to buy the new house you love, you notice that your mortgage lender is charging you over five thousand dollars in origination fees, origination points, application fees, underwriting fees, and various other fees. When you question these fees, the typical response is, "Don't worry about those fees. When you do the math, you'll see that you are actually paying only a few dollars per month for those." Your lender is trying to shift the focus onto cash flow and away from the absolute cost. Put up a fight and say something like, "Yes, I agree that it's not much per month, but I have to borrow five thousand dollars more than I would have otherwise in order to pay those fees. I would be able to take out a smaller loan if I didn't have to pay those fees. And, I'm going to have to pay interest on these costs!"

Show them you understand the game and how the extra costs affect your bottom line. Then anticipate the lender's switch of focus once again to address your latest objection. Your lender may respond, "If you're concerned about raising your loan amount and paying those fees for thirty years, may I suggest you pay the five thousand dollars of fees up front at the time of your settlement? I can redo the paperwork and reduce the loan amount by five thousand dollars, if you want to come out of pocket for these fees." Be ready to respond by saying, "That would help with my monthly payments, but I still want to negotiate the *total amount* of these fees. Whether I pay them now or have them added into the loan amount, I need you to see what you can do to lower the fees. You are doing a great job for me, and I want you to make money, but regardless of when I pay it, five thousand dollars seems like too much money."

30. Double Dipping

Only after you get the best price on one widget should you even bring up the possibility that you may buy more than one. You can reverse the process later. Of course, it's always a good idea to ask for a volume discount if you're purchasing more than one of something, but remember to keep that request in your back pocket only to be used after you have already negotiated the best price you can for one widget. The trick is trying to convince the seller that you would entertain the possibility of buying more than one *only* if it will allow you to get a much better deal.

Let the seller convince you the deal will be much better if you buy more than one widget; try to make it clear that you will not be buying more than the original single widget if there isn't a satisfactory volume discount. Make it appear that the purchase of more than one was not your intention, but is now a remote possibility, if you can see the value and financial sense for doing so.

Once you believe you've negotiated the best price on the first widget, say, "Just out of curiosity, how much would I save on each widget if I bought more than one? If it's worth it, maybe I'll consider it." If the seller agrees to provide you with a volume discount, you have now successfully "double dipped." If you had negotiated for a volume discount first, the seller would have tried to convince you that the bulk discount took into consideration both the best price and also a volume discount on top of it, but you'd never really know whether this was true. Therefore, always ask for each discount separately, and in the correct order, and you can be certain you've done your best to obtain two separate discounts.

31. Damaged Goods Discount

The same principles apply if you are trying to negotiate a discount because something you are buying is damaged. First, negotiate on the price of the item as if it were new and in perfect condition. Once you get the best price, you can double dip by then asking what the discount is because the item is damaged. If you bring up the damage too soon, then it is unlikely that you will get a *second* adjustment for the damage. Again, you cannot go back, so doing things in the right order is crucial.

In the Raphaely way, after you negotiate the best price that you can, you'd say something like, "I think the price is a fair one, but I just started thinking about the damage to the hood of the car. I know we hadn't spoken about it before, but the more I think about it the more I'm thinking I want to negotiate something that allows me to afford to fix this immediately."

The seller's natural reaction, if she's savvy, is that she already factored in the damage. You have to be ready to say something like, "Well, I wasn't really focused on the damage until just now. The price we negotiated wouldn't be good for me if we can't make some sort of adjustment for the damage. I got caught up in our discussions, but now I realize I'm going to have to spend money to get this repaired, so I want to make sure the final price reflects that." Alternatively, if it's obvious that you wouldn't actually be spending money to get the damage fixed, you could say: "I just realized the damage will affect the value when I try to sell this item in the future and, accordingly, I need to make sure the price reflects this so I don't take too great of a loss when I sell."

32. The Other Guy's People

Find out who has the other guy's ear and get them on your side. Don't underestimate the power wielded by people close to the decision-maker. The other side may be consulting with or getting advice from a spouse, business partner, key employee, or some other person during the negotiating process. You want to get to know these people and win them over. If you can get them to trust you and like you or your product it may sway them to side with you on an issue, and convince the decision-maker to work something out with you instead of working things out with someone else.

If you are in negotiations with a team of two people or more, be careful not to belittle, ignore, or offend any of them. Many people will make the common mistake of assuming the most vocal, charismatic, or seemingly most interested individual is the only person you need to win over. Never assume you can pick out the ringleader, the one with the most clout in the group, or the one who is actually the most financially vested in the transaction.

The dynamics of relationships are often very different behind closed doors or among the group itself than what may appear to the outside world. Never rule out any team member as being the key decision maker. The one with the real clout may be shy among strangers but actually lead the group, and be the one with the final say regarding the outcome.

In group meetings make sure you address each person with a reasonable amount of eye contact, attention, and body language. Be responsive to each person's comments, concerns, and questions. Also make sure each person is able to see and understand anything you present or demonstrate to the group. Your lack of attention to one individual could lead to a feeling of alienation. Any resentments will work to your disadvantage come decision time.

33. Meeting Halfway

Always keep in mind the "meet in the middle" negotiation principle while in negotiations. Many people consider a fair and successful negotiation to be one in which two parties start with their respective numbers and then continually "meet in the middle" or "split the difference" over and over, until they end up with a mutually acceptable number. To many people, this process defines "playing fair" and ultimately becomes a major factor in negotiations.

Let's say you are asking $100 for your coffee table, and the potential buyer offers you $50. You reject the offer, and you counteroffer at $90. The buyer then suggests for the two of you to meet in the middle or split the difference between $50 and $90, which would be $70. This may or may not be acceptable to you, but the important thing is that you recognize and anticipate this type of negotiation. It may not be brought up this quickly; it may take someone a couple more rounds of going back and forth before the suggestion is made. Either way, you should be ready for it at all times. If you understand the concept, can anticipate when it may come up, and know how to apply it to your benefit, then you'll win at this type of negotiation each and every time.

In the example above, most people would have probably agreed that $70 was the fair place to meet in the middle. It seems fair, doesn't it? But you saw it coming and know how to apply this type of tactic to your benefit. Your response should be that $70 is *not* meeting in the middle. You can be much craftier with the numbers than this. Technically, the buyer would be right. You started at $100, the buyer offered $50, it was then your turn, at which time you went down to $90, and then the suggestion was made to split the difference, which results in a meeting point of $70. But, because you're much more skilled, you respond by saying, "No, because I was originally at $100. I already went down to $90 because I really thought we'd meet at that number. That was the lowest I was really prepared to go. So if you want to meet in the middle, then the number should be halfway between $100, which was my starting point, and $50, which was your starting point. And that number would be $75 and not $70." It would be difficult for the buyer to disagree with you, and you just earned yourself an extra $5.

Once you become skilled with applying the "split the difference" method of negotiating, you can then be the one to decide how it is used. This is because there will always be different ways to apply it to the numbers. *The trick is in being the one to decide how and when to do the math.* If the buyer was skilled, she'd respond to you by saying, "No, that doesn't seem like the fair way to resolve this, because if you apply that logic, then you also have to keep in mind that I thought we would have agreed on $50. I really wanted to offer $40, but I went higher originally because I was trying to avoid having so many stages of back and forth. So, if we split the difference between my original aim of $40 and your original aim of $100, we'd be at $70." Or, smarter yet, the buyer could say that splitting the difference doesn't work the way in which you are attempting to apply it. You started at $100, she went to $50, and you went to $90 because it was your turn to give a number. Once you went down to $90 that became your new number and it's now unfair for you to once again bring up your old number of $100 because that makes her feel like she's negotiating against herself.

Now that you understand the "meet in the middle" concept and see how it can be applied in various ways, you will be aware of and stay ahead of it while negotiating. If you sense you're dealing with someone who will be applying this type of reasoning in his or her negotiating, be extra careful with your numbers. If selling, keep your numbers consistently higher than you originally would have during every round of negotiations because these numbers will be the starting point for splitting the difference when that time comes.

Try not to be the one to suggest the "meet in the middle" solution to a negotiation. Anyone offering this type of solution is essentially tipping her hat that she's willing to adjust her number to that "meet in the middle" price she suggests. If she wasn't okay with adjusting her number up or down to that amount, then she would have never suggested "meet in the middle" to begin with.

For example, if you are selling your car for $10,000, and the buyer is offering $9,000, you are obviously $1,000 apart. If the buyer offers to "meet in the middle" to resolve the difference, he has just informed you he is willing to pay $9,500. He has essentially raised his offer from $9,000 to $9,500. If you're okay with accepting $9,500, then you will come across as accommodating and wanting to be reasonable to get the deal done. If, however, you don't want to go down to $9,500, you could just agree to go down to $9,800 or whatever number above $9,500 you wish. He's now gone up $500, but you've only adjusted your price by $200. You are at an advantage in the final stages of this negotiation because *he* suggested the "meet in the middle."

Only when you've reached the final stages do you do your best to get the other guy to make the "meet in the middle" suggestion. Say something like, "We're $1,000 apart. What should we do now?" Let him offer meeting in the middle at $9,500, and you have led him into adapting that as his new number! He won't even realize what is happening. You take his suggestion and come back with something like this: "Since you're at $9,500 and I'm at $10,000, let's just meet in the middle at $9,750." Good work!

34. Exploring Options

Unless you are contractually precluded from doing so, don't shut down or turn away other similar opportunities that may arise or become known to you just because you are already in negotiations. Exploring other options could end up protecting your interests in the event the original party changes his or her mind and rejects your deal. Additionally, exploring other options may provide you with helpful insight into the current deal you're negotiating.

It's possible that the current deal you're negotiating starts off looking great but becomes less and less attractive as more of its details become available to you. And it's also possible that other options out there may appear unappealing at first glance but actually become more interesting and appealing when the details become known to you. You never know when the apparent long shot could become your best bet at the end of the day.

35. Demonstrate Your Other Options

Place yourself in a position of power. Demonstrate to the other side that you have options. Make them aware you are also in talks with a competitor, or that there are other potential buyers who are interested in what you're selling. Explain to a realtor who is charging 3 percent commission that you were approached by other realtors who are offering to charge only 2 percent. Anticipate the realtor's likely responses: "You get what you pay for. I have much more experience than those other realtors, so I'm worth the higher rate." You may agree, but that doesn't mean you have to let the realtor know it. Counter whatever argument is being made; turn the perceived disadvantage of your other option into a positive to convince your audience that the other option is a viable alternative for you. "Yes, the other realtors have less experience than you do, but I like that, because I know they're very hungry and want to prove themselves." When the realtor sees that her contentions have not deterred you from exploring other options, she has to seriously consider lowering her commissions or facing the risk of losing you as a client.

When purchasing an item, let the seller know that you have something similar you're also looking at. Some embellishment is good. "I really like your car, but it's a tough choice because the other car has really low mileage." "I like your boat, but the other boat has the most perfect cabins I've seen on a boat this size." Try turning something lacking on the item you are negotiating about into a big advantage for the competition. "Your kitchen is so nice, but the other house has all stainless-steel appliances, which I just love."

Be careful not to overdo it, and never become overcritical or insulting. Just put it out there once or twice so they know you have options that are just as good. Be ready for the possible question: "If you like the other house so much, why don't you buy that one?" Your response should impress upon the other party that you haven't necessarily picked a favorite, that both (or more) options present you with great features, but ultimately the price and terms will be critical factors in your decision.

36. Know the Other Side's Options

If they don't work things out with you, what are their options? Are there other people offering the same services or selling the same item you are? Do you have any leverage? Are you or your offer unique in any way? Be realistic in these assessments. You can ask the other side about their options, just as you would have asked sellers about any other offers they've received on the item they're selling. While discussing the deal you're working out, you can always ask something like: "If we don't work things out, what would you do? Are you going to be buying a snowblower like this regardless of whether we work something out, or would you just hold off altogether for now?" If you are selling your house, you could ask: "Are there other houses you're looking at currently?"

The exact questions you ask will obviously depend on the circumstances and on what sort of item you are negotiating Never be afraid to ask these types of questions. If you ask your questions correctly, it will come across as if you are simply inquiring in a friendly manner while making conversation. If the people on the other side are uncomfortable answering these types of questions, they'll let you know they prefer to keep that information private. Don't be offended if they respond in this manner, as some people aren't comfortable revealing these types of details. Some people may also not be completely truthful with the information they provide, so do your best at assessing the person's credibility, and do a good job of listening carefully for contradictions in his or her details. Ultimately, you will gain valuable information and insight more often than not by asking for these specifics, and you'll be able to apply it to your assessment of how aggressively you should negotiate.

37. Create Competition

Get their competitive juices flowing. Are you an employee being recruited by several companies? If so, it would be beneficial for you to make each of these companies aware of this, as one company may want to make a more enticing offer to you to make sure its competitor doesn't hire you. But you must do this carefully. You don't want to turn people off by coming across as arrogant or making them feel like you are intentionally pitting the companies against each other to your benefit.

When considering multiple opportunities, refer to other offers in the context of needing clarification on the terms and benefits offered by the employer you are currently meeting with. Make it seem as if you're having a difficult time making your choice between two companies, but be sure to emphasize to the interviewer that you really like this company and that you're hoping to go with them. If it appears that you're just holding out for whoever does more for you, you will lose their trust. Be convincing that it's partly about the intangibles for you, such as the personalities of the individuals with whom you'd be working, the work atmosphere, or the vision and goals of that company. A company's knowledge that its competitors are actively pursuing you will generally make it more likely that it willl offer you more than it would have otherwise.

If you are buying a home, it would be helpful to your situation if the sellers of the house you really like are aware that you are also considering the house down the street from them. If you seem like a serious buyer, they don't want to lose the opportunity to one of their neighbors.

If you are in the process of negotiating with a vendor on the purchase of a product or service, and you're getting quotes from several vendors, find out whether they know each other. Do they often go head to head when trying to land new clients? Have they developed a strongly competitive relationship? How can you benefit from this situation? Develop a bidding frenzy. Do your best to remind them of the other guy when you can. When they realize they're being compared head-on with their competitors, your account will begin to take on a bigger meaning to each of them. If you choose to do business with one vendor over the other, what result would that have on the morale of the losing competitor?

Don't underestimate any of these factors. Sometimes vendors can get so wrapped up in beating the other guy, rallying their troops, "winning," or receiving validation that they end up throwing in everything but the kitchen sink in the process. Do your best to discover potential situations like this and pounce!

38. Know When to Walk Away

Have you ever been told that you can't always get what you want? If it means too much to you, then you are not going to get a good deal. Wanting something too badly hurts your ability to negotiate. You won't be able to take any risks, bluff, or take your time. You lose lots of leverage. Try to convince yourself that other opportunities like this one *will* come around again.

You need to remember back to an earlier time when you felt like you just had to have something at any cost. After some time passed, was it really as critical to you to get that item or deal as you originally had thought? With the benefit of hindsight, you now see that life would have gone on without it.

At some point, you have to be able to tell yourself it wasn't meant to be and walk away from a bad deal, a deal in which you feel that you're being forced to pay more or accept less than you believe you should. If you cannot convince yourself that you can live without this deal, then you have to accept the fact that you will probably not get a great deal. Now is the time to turn your focus on doing your best to utilize as many of the tools of a skilled negotiator as you can.

39. Dealing with Deadlines

Don't be intimidated by deadlines. Deadlines come and go. Take your time, make good choices, and try not to make decisions if you have to rush. Sometimes the best decision is to make no decision at all, or to simply pass on an opportunity. If it's meant to be, somehow miraculously the deal will still be available after the deadline passes. No matter what they tell you at the time to try to get you to cooperate with their deadline, parties rarely take back their offer or give you a worse offer just because some deadline has passed. Likewise, parties rarely raise a price or provide you with worse service just because some deadline has passed. However, exceptions to this obviously exist in cases in which there truly is limited inventory or limited time by which to complete a task or service.

If you are convinced this deadline will represent a true end to the opportunity, then do your best to fulfill the obligations of the deadline, but only after you are satisfied you've had ample time to analyze the situation properly. First, gather all information so that you can intelligently determine whether you are, in fact, dealing with a legitimate deadline. What happens if the deadline passes? Does the food spoil? Does the weather change? Will ownership of the item automatically pass on to someone else by operation of law? Will their unemployment or other benefits be cut off? Will their car warranty expire? Will their lease term end? Are they rushing because they're hiding something? Do they want to deprive you of sufficient time to gather all of the facts? After analysis, if you determine that the deadline was legitimate, and the other side is facing a fairly desperate time-related situation, this will help you in your negotiations.

If there is no indication that the deadline is a result of any such events, then it's very possible that the deadline can be modified, therefore providing you with additional time in which to make your decision and negotiate the terms in your favor. People sometimes impose deadlines on themselves and others because they know things frequently take longer than anticipated at first, and the deadlines are good methods by which to try to keep those time overruns at a minimum. Slowing things down can lead to additional concessions in the hopes of getting the deal done. You will see the people on the other side begin to negotiate against themselves as this takes place. The more you slow things down, the more likely the other side will keep offering you a better deal to prevent the risk of losing the deal altogether.

40. Negotiating Salary

Try to get the employer to provide a number regarding compensation *first*, before you have to. You are at a disadvantage if you provide numbers before the employer does, because now the employer can modify his or her numbers based on your expectations.

It's easy to suggest you can just go into an interview and turn the tables on your interviewer when you are asked about salary requirements. In reality, when in this situation, you are probably scared and nervous enough without trying to be aggressive when it comes to compensation. You don't want to seem arrogant, evasive, or disrespectful as you try to turn the question back on them when asked about salary.

So how exactly do you accomplish this tough task? It's simpler than you might imagine. When asked about your salary requirements, respond with something like this: "I want to be compensated an amount you have in mind for this position for someone with my qualifications and experience." Or you can ask something like, "What is a normal range for this position for someone with my qualifications?" If you handle this "turnaround" in a polite, nonconfrontational manner, the employer may give in and provide you with a number or range. If you successfully manage to make this happen, you have done yourself a great service and potentially earned yourself thousands of additional dollars in salary. You never know if a number you would have given your interviewers would have been lower than the number or range they provide to you, and you'll never know if you don't try to get them to provide that information first.

41. Potential Employees

Stay up-to-date with starting salaries and ongoing salaries in your industry, as you need to know what the competition is paying. You have to make sure you know what's standard in your industry for each position and what candidates expect to get paid. Additionally, you must assess the type of market conditions that currently exist. Is everyone desperately searching for employees? Or is the market outlook not good and candidates are fortunate to find a job in your industry at the current time?

Don't assume the candidate you are interviewing knows as much as you do about the market conditions or average starting salaries. The candidate may only be using his or her own experiences in determining the expected or normal salary, whereas you have already interviewed and hired dozens of people. Accordingly, don't assume what the candidate wants or expects to be paid. You should always ask.

Don't go first! You will often be surprised that the candidate's requested number is substantially less than the number you thought this individual would settle for. Try to get his or her expected or desired salary before you provide any salary information.

You may be prepared to pay $40,000 for this position, but this person may be coming to you after having worked at two previous companies where she was severely underpaid. If that's the case, she may have been getting paid only $25,000 in each of her last jobs even though the majority of companies pay much more for that position and that level of experience. If that's the case, you could offer $30,000 and she would probably be very appreciative. You just saved $10,000 annually because you let her speak and divulge her number first.

Obviously, this assumes she and your other employees don't share private salary information once she joins the team, or if they do, that your employees understand each person gets paid differently depending on various criteria. Remember, however, if she approaches you in several weeks or months and asks for more money, you could always raise her salary at that time. At least in the meantime you've saved that difference, and you had a chance to assess her performance and qualifications before paying her more.

Get to the candidate's bottom line quickly. If you are interviewing potential employees, it is a good practice to ask them what their current salary is or what they "need" to make early in the meeting. If the person is currently unemployed, ask what he or she made in previous jobs.

Here's a good strategy if the job market is bad. You ask, "What is the absolute lowest you can afford to accept to start off, with the knowledge that we can reassess after a short probationary period?" Once you receive your answer, you'll often be surprised to hear it can be substantially less than what you expected it would be. You've made it clear that this starting salary is temporary until they've proven themselves. This saves you money until that probationary period is over, and it will cause them to be more appreciative of the higher salary you may agree to after the probationary period.

There is another very good reason to pay less during a probationary period and then agree to a higher salary after the new employee has proven himself or herself. Let's assume you would have paid this new employee $40,000 per year, but you and the employee agreed on a starting salary of $30,000 during a three-month probationary period with a reassessment after the probationary period. After three months pass, you agree to pay the employee forty thousand dollars going forward, which again is what you would have gladly paid from the beginning anyway, if you weren't a skilled negotiator. Is your new employee as likely to come to you again anytime soon asking for another raise? The answer is no. People usually have their own time frames for when and why it's appropriate to ask their employer for a raise. In their mind, they have basically already asked for, and received, their first raise.

Lastly, unless you are offering an insane amount of money, don't include salary information in employment advertisements. If you do so, you're committing yourself to paying at least that much when chances are you may have been able to pay less for many of the potential applicants. The only time you should actually publicize salary information is if it's high enough that you think it will attract much more attention to your advertisement. If it's not high enough to provide for that additional interest level, then don't commit yourself to a number in advance.

42. Negotiating with Vendors

Your goal is to convince a vendor that you will be a potential regular or return customer. Vendors will be more likely to offer you discounts or additional services if they think you'll buy from them again. They will be more likely to give you a break if they can see that you will be loyal and appreciative when they do so. Show them you have respect for their time, products, and services. Make it clear that you appreciate what they're doing for you and that you will spread the word to others and help them get future business from other people. Show them you are someone they want to treat well and make exceptions for, because you can be a great connector for them.

If you're in business and negotiating with a vendor, demonstrate your company is growing and that this is only the beginning. Every vendor hopes to find that starting small business that is poised for growth so he will in turn receive more and more business from you.

43. Negotiating with Customers

When dealing with clients or customers, whenever possible try to foster an atmosphere in which customers feel like they are involved in the determination of their pricing. With a potential client who is comparing your products or services with those of competitors, create an atmosphere of trust and cooperation by requesting that this future customer provide you with a final opportunity to beat other offers. It is vital for the potential customer to *allow you to be last in line for quotes.*

Let's assume you own a roofing company. You have been contacted by the operators of a strip mall looking to hire a company like yours to replace the roof. They have informed you that they are speaking with three other roofing companies similar to yours with similar reputations, abilities, and experience, and that their decision will be made solely based on price. They are requesting quotes from each company and will ultimately hire the company that provides the lowest quote. None of the companies will know anything about the quotes provided by its competitors.

Obviously you need to agree to this request. But, you can do something else the others may not do if they are not skilled negotiators. Develop a good rapport with these potential clients, and request permission to have another chance to revise your bid should you end up not being the lowest bidder. If you aren't the lowest bidder, they will share with you the specific number of the lowest bid, along with all of its details so you could review it, because otherwise you'd be forced to merely take their word for it. Do you think any of the other companies would think of making this same request? Probably not, but a skilled negotiator is always looking for his or her edge!

44. Which Side Wants It More

Look for clues as to how serious, pressured, desperate, or eager the people on the other side are to work through a deal with you. Are they going out of their way to meet with you? Are they spending a seemingly great amount of money to come to you or to get you to come to meet them? If it appears that they are *too* eager to work out an agreement with you, make sure you take that into consideration as you negotiate. They may be willing to give up more than you originally thought.

How did you and the other individual come to find each

other? If he or she found you, is that an indication that he or she is eager to do a deal with you? If negotiations are taking place over time, are you noticing that he or she is initiating contact more now than the individual did before? Could this be a sign that he or she is more interested now, or that another option he or she was pursuing did not work out?

Keep in mind, of course, that you must be objective as you conduct this assessment. You don't want to misinterpret their customary hustle for excess eagerness to do a deal with you.

45. Assess Pressures

Is the other guy facing some immediate pressures that could provide you with an advantage? Are you negotiating with a potential employee who just lost his or her job and is now unemployed? Are you negotiating your starting salary and compensation package with a company that just lost a key employee? Are you negotiating the monthly rental amount with landlords who desperately need to rent their house because they are facing an imminent foreclosure? Are you negotiating with a vendor who was just turned down by all of your competitors and, therefore, you represent the vendor's final hope for making a deal?

This isn't a suggestion to take advantage of people in tough situations; rather, it's just a reminder to always do your homework. Even in the final stages of a negotiation, there may be immediate pressures that could affect how badly the other side needs to make a deal. Knowing the other side is facing a fairly desperate situation allows you to be more comfortable in standing your ground and sticking to your guns.

Be careful, however, not to make unreasonable demands because you think the people on the other side have no choice. When you begin to be unreasonable, you lose out on potential good deals. They may decide to suffer the consequences of

making no deal at all, or become very resourceful in searching
for alternatives because of your difficult behavior.

CHAPTER SIX

Understanding and Using Precedents

Precedents are a cornerstone of many negotiations and deserve special consideration. Read on to discover why.

1. Understanding Precedents

Both parties to a deal often use a similar incident, transaction, or item as a precedent to determine the value of the current item or service being negotiated. Make yourself aware of relevant precedents; try to be aware of what precedents the other party may bring up. Finally, understand how to assess precedents so that they're interpreted in your favor during the current negotiation.

Let's assume you are a house painter. Potential clients are requesting an estimate from you because you painted their neighbor's house a month ago. It is likely that they know exactly how much you charged to paint the other house. You know that you should have charged much more money for that job and you don't want to make the same mistake twice. When you provide these new clients with a higher estimate, of course they are going to ask why you're charging more. How will you differentiate the price you gave their neighbor compared with the price you are charging them? You could point out to the new clients that they have more furniture to move out of the way, or that their house is not as easy to paint for one reason or another, or that your costs of labor or material have gone up since you painted their neighbor's house, and so forth.

2. Caution Before Setting Those Precedents

Always keep in mind that if you are negotiating with someone you may negotiate with in the future, he or she will remember everything that takes place during the current situation, and it will set the stage. For example, if you quickly accept much less than you originally asked for during a negotiation, the other party will remember that your first number is meaningless and that there is plenty of wiggle room between that number and what you will finally agree to accept. If you agree to resolve a negotiation by "meeting in the middle," you are potentially setting *that* precedent.

3. The Slippery Slope

Once you let the other side become accustomed to something at a certain level, it is important to realize that any deviation from that level sets the bar at a notch below. Let's assume your dentist charges about 5 percent more each year. Your twice-yearly checkup started at $100 per visit and has consistently increased, by these small increments, and that bar continues to be reset time and again. When the dentist raised the price to $105, you didn't mind because it was such a minor change. You then became comfortable at the $105 price point, but then the dentist raised the prices again, this time to $110. You again didn't mind very much because it represented such a small change from $105, which had become the new price standard. You probably already had forgotten that the price had originally been $100 and, instead, you simply compared the revised price of $110 to your then current price of $105, at which time you determined the change was minor and you were satisfied with it. This trend continued consistently because you allowed the slippery slope to begin and continue. If you continue to allow the price to rise, eventually you'll get to a point where it may be too late to get things under control.

Standard lease agreements typically contain such small, incremental increases. These leases may provide for a small, incremental increase of 3 percent in the total rent. That increase may not seem like a large amount, but it certainly adds up to a lot of money after several years.

Do your best to put up a good battle when even minor price or service changes or concessions are asked of you in an ongoing relationship. Remember that this individual is storing that information and it will set the tone for future negotiations.

4. Take Advantage of Other Precedents

Have you ever negotiated with these individuals before? Do you know anyone else who has had any negotiations or business dealings with them? Recall or obtain as much information in advance as you can, as it can prove very useful to you. Do they present their best and final offer at the very beginning, expecting you either to take or leave it? Or do they start negotiations with a number far off from their final number, thereby building in much cushion for back-and-forth negotiations? What has motivated them in the past? Was it money, ego, or something else?

5. Consider the Other Side's Fear of Precedent

Are you trying to get a job with an employer and, as you discuss salary, you realize your interviewers may be concerned about not paying you more than a certain range because knowledge of your salary by other employees could potentially cause them to feel forced to give other employees substantial raises? Your awareness of their concern allows you to help them think of ways around this issue. Can they pay you part of your salary in bonuses instead? Can they allow you additional vacation time or provide you with extra benefits or reimbursements to make up for a lower salary? If you didn't know to listen for clues regarding this issue, you may have just concluded they don't want to hire you or they aren't willing to recognize your true value. By asking the right questions and finding out more facts, you have armed yourself with this knowledge, and you can help suggest these other options that may allow for the deal to get done.

Does it seem as if your realtor would agree to lower her commission to 1 percent on your particular transaction but cannot do so because she's concerned that, if others discovered this, she'd be expected to lower her commission for other future clients as well? Do you sense the maid service that cleans most of the houses in your neighborhood would be willing to charge you less than she charges your neighbors because she needs business but is afraid to change her prices? How can you creatively come up with a way to get discounted pricing from the realtor or the maid service? How about offering to sign a nondisclosure agreement, by which you would be precluded from sharing the details with anyone? Or is there another way by which you can achieve the cost savings while no precedent is set? The realtor can charge you her normal commission rate and then provide additional services that she may not normally offer her clients. The maid service can also make up the difference to you by providing additional services at no additional cost.

CHAPTER SEVEN

Cooperation not Competition

As the deal closes, in the final stages of negotiation it is critical to create an atmosphere of connection and mutual satisfaction while remaining alert for further opportunity.

1. Appeal to Their Emotions

Keep in mind: You have to do a good job of getting your way without hurting the other person's pride or ego. How do you do that? You have to give him or her something to hang his or her hat on. You divert the attention from the bottom line to something else that will allow him or her to feel like he or she didn't get taken advantage of. Can you thank the individual for giving in to you on certain issues and convince this person you owe him or her and therefore next time he or she will get a better bargain from you as a result? Do your best to understand these people. What motivates them? Is it recognition? If so, you could possibly offer recognition in front of their peers, if they are willing to make some concessions you're requesting. Or is praise more important? Would these people accept less if they receive praise for doing the right thing or for being reasonable? Are they concerned about being able to envision a compelling future for themselves? Are you able to demonstrate to them that they may not be getting exactly what they wanted but, as a result, they are creating a more exciting future for themselves? Are they motivated by friendship? Would they be willing to give in or accept less than they wanted in the hopes of earning the opportunity to be your friends as a result?

2. Don't Make People Feel Powerless

If an individual feels like he or she was powerless and that you essentially got your way without offering him or her a choice, you will not win in the end. Powerlessness leads to feelings of resentment. He or she will either find any way possible to change terms after the fact, or you won't receive the full performance when all is said and done.

3. Avoid Condescension and Insults

When you disagree with the other party, do so in a respectful, inoffensive way. Never be pompous or arrogant. Doing so will ensure that the other person will do everything in his or her power to "prove you wrong" and get even. When you act in a condescending manner by attacking the other person's self-image, you can only cause offense or anger.

The trick is to check your own ego at the door while relaxing and reassuring the other party's ego. Be careful not to awaken this sleeping giant, because concluding the negotiation will become more difficult if you do so.

4. Be Likable

People do business with people they like, they buy from people they like, and they give in or give the benefit of the doubt to people they like. People will do more, help more, and give up more for people they like. Be polite, engaging, and deferential whenever possible. You can be likeable while still standing your ground, playing hardball, or disagreeing with the other party. You certainly have to be able to stand up for yourself and be assertive, but do so respectfully without offending the other party. Others may see that you are tough, demanding, or shrewd, but as long as your demeanor is still friendly and respectful, they will be able to continue to like you even if you are being tough on them during the course of your negotiations.

5. Put Yourself in Their Shoes

When you do your best to put yourself in other people's shoes, it becomes easier to keep your cool and understand where they're coming from even if they aren't appearing reasonable at the time. As with all aspects of your life, try to see the good in other people and always remind yourself they are just doing the best they can with the emotional and intellectual resources they have available.

As long as you don't take things personally, you will be less likely to react with anger or get rattled. Consequently, you'll be more patient and will foster an atmosphere more likely to promote collaboration and conversation instead of confrontation.

6. Appeal to Their Desire to be Caring

It doesn't hurt to bring up that you're a struggling, single parent, that you're paying your own way through college, or that you're just getting started in business on a shoestring budget. People like helping others in these types of situations. If the people on the other side can go home to their partners and say that more was spent than they had discussed, but a struggling artist or a person who is rebuilding was helped, then you may get the benefit of the doubt during your negotiations.

Be truthful and don't take advantage of peoples' good nature, but don't be afraid to bring up these honest "in need" factors and make the other person aware of your situation. Naturally, don't use this when dealing with someone who is less fortunate than you, but certainly don't be afraid of using it when dealing with someone who, in your assessment, can afford to be helpful to you while you're in the midst of tough times.

7. Collaboration

Create an atmosphere in which there is a feeling you are working together. Show your counterparts you are working with them and not against them. Change the perception of the negotiation from a conflict between the parties to a problem or situation the parties are working on together to resolve. Your handling of the situation in this manner should eventually lead to the other party's feeling and acting in a similar fashion. The only thing preventing you from agreeing are the details of the deal, and you will keep working out these differences until you are on the same page.

8. Create Connection

While you negotiate, create a personal connection. Try to get the person you are dealing with to develop an interest in your well-being and goals. This will foster an atmosphere of cooperation, as you learn more about the other person's motivation, goals, tactics, and conversation style.

Small talk leads to big things. Utilize opportunities to speak with people. Maintain a positive attitude, which will put the other party at ease and promote an atmosphere in which everyone believes his or her goals are being accomplished.

9. Make a New Friend

When you need assistance from a store clerk, the other side in a negotiation, a restaurant hostess, or any individual from whom you are trying to get help, you should work at enlisting that person as your ally. Acknowledging them as people able to support and assist you empowers them and makes them more likely to help you.

People generally enjoy helping others in a tough situation, but remember you're most likely to get their assistance if you make your request in a skillful manner. Don't make your request look like you're simply begging or pleading, and that it's all about you and your needs. Instead, demonstrate you are a sincere and appreciative person.

10. Demonstrate Your Value

Demonstrate you are someone worthy of extra attention or consideration. Can you show the vendor that you are a *connector*, and that you can refer his or her services to many other people? Can you show your boss that it's good business to give you a raise because of all that you bring to the table for the company? You are too valuable to lose as an employee. Show the hostess at the restaurant that you are someone the restaurant wants as part of its clientele. Demonstrate to the store manager you are a person the store wants as a regular customer. Remember usually the only way by which you will receive help from anyone is if you ask.

11. Get That Discount

Ask for a discount and frame it in a charming and joking manner. You have nothing to lose this way. If the other people can't negotiate or aren't yet ready to do so, then they'll most likely laugh it off and tell you they wish they could lower the price for you. The key is if they are open to giving you a discount or negotiating with you, then you've opened the door for those talks.

You can ask for "the good customer discount." You can ask to be upgraded to the presidential suite. You can ask for the "new to town" discount, the "first time in New York discount," or the "Marriott is my favorite hotel" discount. After you have made some small talk, there is the "now that we go so far back" discount. There's the good old "friends and family discount" because now that you've been speaking for a couple of minutes you are like family. You could say to the front-desk clerk something like, "This is really a nice hotel. Do you own this place? I can tell you are the one who makes all of the decisions around here." The main ingredients in this approach are being friendly and having a sense of humor.

CHAPTER EIGHT

Hail and Farewell!

Congratulations! You have just completed the course work for the Raphaely School for Skilled Negotiators! You now see opportunities and solutions where others see problems and dead ends. You understand and appreciate that much of your everyday life is a negotiation, and you embrace tough situations because you are confident in your problem-solving, negotiating, and people skills. You are quick to recognize the perspective of others, which allows you to understand their wants and needs, therefore making it easier for you to identify creative solutions to everyday situations. You come up with potential solutions by collecting relevant data so that you know the facts involved, by thinking outside the box, and by creatively formulating multiple resolutions when others see none. Your perspective, confidence, and skills allow you to sail smoothly through your daily life while others may experience frustration. Your new way of thinking makes your entire life, your relationships, and your business dealings more pleasurable, less stressful, and more rewarding.

From now on, you will view all situations with others as

potential opportunities to further develop your skills, and you will notice these skills continuing to improve almost daily. In order to truly graduate, you will need to apply these principles to the real-life situations that lie ahead. You may need to refer back to sections of this book for a refresher class.

As a final reminder, always keep in mind the following fifteen basic principles of a skilled negotiator:

1. Slow things down; negotiations are marathons and not sprints.

2. Speak less and listen more.

3. Don't interrupt the other side.

4. Go last; he or she who speaks first loses.

5. Never make the other guy feel like he lost.

6. View a negotiation as a series of steps and not as one action.

7. Be respectful, polite, and likable.

8. Think outside the box; come up with creative solutions.

9. Always come prepared.

10. Never assume anything.

11. Ask for what you want.

12. Keep on trying; don't give up.

13. Ask a lot of questions.

14. Never start with your best, bottom-line number.

15. Always make the other side feel satisfied with the deal.

Good luck to you in your future endeavors! Remember what you have learned, do your best to maintain a positive and optimistic outlook, and, most of all, enjoy all of the great experiences life has to offer.

May you win all of life's negotiations!

Made in the USA
Middletown, DE
28 May 2020

96205180R00064